PENGUIN STUDY GUI
The Caucasian Chalk Circl

Sabine Gross was educated at the universities of Heidelberg, Frankfurt and Santa Barbara-California. She is a professor of modern German literature and of theatre at the University of Wisconsin-Madison. She has contributed to the *Bertolt Brecht Reference Companion*, the *Brecht Yearbook* and the *Communications* of the *International Brecht Society*, of which she is a member. She has written extensively on twentieth-century authors, and has directed a number of student productions.

Bertold Brecht (1898–1956) is one of Germany's best-known playwrights. His social critiques, including *The Caucasian Chalk Circle*, *Mother Courage and Her Children* and *The Threepenny Opera*, resonate with modern audiences and continue to be frequently performed.

Penguin Study Guide

The Caucasian Chalk Circle

BERTOLT BRECHT

Sabine Gross

PENGUIN BOOKS

PENGUIN BOOKS

Published by the Penguin Group
Penguin Books Ltd, 80 Strand, London WC2R 0RL, England
Penguin Group (USA) Inc., 375 Hudson Street, New York, New York 10014, USA
Penguin Group (Canada), 90 Eglinton Avenue East, Suite 700, Toronto, Ontario, Canada M4P 2Y3
(a division of Pearson Penguin Canada Inc.)
Penguin Ireland, 25 St Stephen's Green, Dublin 2, Ireland (a division of Penguin Books Ltd)
Penguin Group (Australia), 707 Collins Street, Melbourne, Victoria 3008, Australia
(a division of Pearson Australia Group Pty Ltd)
Penguin Books India Pvt Ltd, 11 Community Centre, Panchsheel Park, New Delhi – 110 017, India
Penguin Group (NZ), 67 Apollo Drive, Rosedale, Auckland 0632, New Zealand
(a division of Pearson New Zealand Ltd)
Penguin Books (South Africa) (Pty) Ltd, Block D, Rosebank Office Park,
181 Jan Smuts Avenue, Parktown North, Gauteng 2193, South Africa

Penguin Books Ltd, Registered Offices: 80 Strand, London WC2R 0RL, England

www.penguin.com

Published in Penguin Books 2014
001

Copyright © Sabine Gross, 2014

The moral right of the author has been asserted

All rights reserved
Without limiting the rights under copyright
reserved above, no part of this publication may be
reproduced, stored in or introduced into a retrieval system,
or transmitted, in any form or by any means (electronic, mechanical,
photocopying, recording or otherwise), without the prior
written permission of both the copyright owner and
the above publisher of this book

Set in 10.3/14 pt Warnock Pro
Typeset by Jouve (UK), Milton Keynes
Printed in Great Britain by Clays Ltd, St Ives plc

A CIP catalogue record for this book is available from the British Library

ISBN: 978-0-141-39692-7

www.greenpenguin.co.uk

MIX
Paper from
responsible sources
FSC® C018179

Penguin Books is committed to a sustainable
future for our business, our readers and our planet.
This book is made from Forest Stewardship
Council™ certified paper.

Contents

To the Student   vii

Introduction: Note on the Author's
Biography and Writing of the Play   1

Synopsis   7

Scene-by-Scene Analysis and Commentary   17

Brecht's 'Epic Theatre': An Overview   67

The Caucasian Chalk Circle
as Brechtian Theatre   81

Conclusion: Major Themes and
Overall Interpretation   111

Discussion Topics and
Examination Questions   121

To the Student

This book is designed to help you with your studies and examinations. It contains a synopsis and a detailed scene-by-scene analysis and commentary, an introduction to Brechtian theatre and notes on the play in the light of Brechtian theatre, as well as a conclusion summarizing major themes and offering an overall interpretation. Information on the author's biography and the writing of the play is also included. Page references are to the Penguin Modern Classics approved school edition translated by Eric Bentley.

When you use this book, remember that it is intended as an aid to your study of the play. It will help you find important passages quickly, deepen your understanding as you read and perhaps give you some ideas for essays. But it is not a substitute for reading the play, and your response to the play and opinions are the things that matter. These are what the examiners are looking for, and they are also what will give you the most pleasure. Show your knowledge and appreciation to the examiner, and show them clearly.

Introduction: Note on the Author's Biography and Writing of the Play

The author

Bertolt Brecht is a major literary figure of the twentieth century. Controversial throughout his life – in his writings, his views on theatre, his politics and his collaborations with others – he is one of the most significant and influential playwrights of our times. He was a prolific writer and his complete works include many different genres, most important among them plays such as *The Caucasian Chalk Circle*, a large number of poems and many essays and theoretical works about theatre and art. He has also written short and long prose narratives and numerous essays on a variety of topics. His 'working diaries' and letters have been published and provide additional insights into his life and work.

On 10 February 1898 Eugen Berthold Friedrich Brecht was born into a stable and prosperous middle-class bourgeois family in Augsburg in southern Germany. He started writing poetry and other texts around the age of sixteen, while still in the *Gymnasium*, the highest level of German schools. A little later he discarded his given name Eugen and from then on called himself Bertolt (or Bert) Brecht. In 1914 the First World War broke out and irrevocably changed the political and social landscape in Germany and internationally. Even at the age of eighteen, Brecht distrusted established authority and uncritically accepted values. He was punished for writing a sharply critical school essay against the dominant patriotic view that it was 'sweet and honourable' to die for one's country. Brecht's artistic talents also included music, and he wrote not just poems but many songs and ballads that he performed himself with the guitar.

After graduating from the *Gymnasium*, Brecht enrolled as a student at the University of Munich in 1918. The next few years were a time of literary experimentation for him: he wrote theatre reviews and his first plays. In the early 1920s, during the post-war years of political unrest his first plays were performed. Brecht's personal life was unsettled and did not conform to bourgeois morality (which he also questioned throughout his life): within a period of five years, from 1919 to 1924, he had three children with three different women. In 1929 he married Helene Weigel, mother of his son Stefan (and in 1930 his daughter Barbara). Weigel was a gifted actress who would perform in many of Brecht's plays; she was an important theatrical collaborator for him and upheld his legacy after his death.

In the late 1920s, as Germany became more politically split, Brecht began to study Marxism and claimed that it helped him to understand the plays he was writing. He believed – along with many others during these early years of the Soviet Union – that communism presented the best political model for the happiness of humankind. Many of his plays and their stage performances were controversial for aesthetic as well as political reasons. His *Threepenny Opera*, based on an eighteenth-century English text, was a major success in 1928. Intended as a critique of bourgeois morality and capitalist economics, it became a crowd-pleaser.

Starting early on in his writing life, Brecht practised a collaborative way of working. He developed ideas and texts in discussions with others, worked with musicians who composed music for his plays, and liked to surround himself with helpers (mostly female – several of them also became his lovers) who did much of the actual work of producing clean copies and correcting his texts for him. He was an exceptionally well-read and original thinker in addition to being a versatile and profoundly gifted writer. Others were attracted to his ideas and projects and willingly joined him. But he was not above exploiting those who worked with him and there were numerous conflicts in his collaborations – about finances, artistic control and the use of materials from other writers – several of which resulted in lawsuits.

Brecht thought of everything as a work-in-progress and kept revising his texts, including his plays, throughout his life. Many were published in multiple versions, so that we frequently see several versions of the same play. For Brecht, the process of working on – and thinking through – his texts was more important than coming up with a finished product, and he was always willing to change things based on discussions with his collaborators and the actors, and also depending on what an individual production in a specific theatre might need.

In the late 1920s Brecht increasingly thought of theatre as a way of changing society and moved away from the Western model of theatre as a vehicle of aesthetic pleasure for the passive enjoyment of middle-class spectators (Brecht called this 'culinary theatre'). Around 1930 he radicalized his thoughts by writing 'learning plays' that were intended primarily for the education of the participants, although several were also performed publicly. He also began developing his thoughts about an 'epic' form of theatre (see the chapter 'Brecht's 'Epic Theatre': An Overview').

In 1933, when Hitler and the National Socialists came to

power in Germany, Brecht and his family fled immediately, since Brecht was considered an enemy of the new fascist regime because of his communist views and political theatre. In one of his most famous poems, 'To Those Born After', Brecht summed up the years of exile that followed – until 1947 – by stating that they changed countries more often than they changed their shoes. While still in Europe, he travelled widely, and his plays were performed in Paris, New York, Copenhagen and Zurich. The years of exile included residencies in Denmark (1939), Sweden and Finland (1939–41, during the first phase of the Second World War) and the USA (1941–7), where he also worked on films in Hollywood. A number of Brecht's major plays were written in exile, among them *Mother Courage*, *The Good Woman of Setzuan* and *Life of Galileo*.

Right before he planned to return to Europe in 1947, Brecht was interrogated by a congressional committee in the USA about his communist leanings. Two years after the end of the Second World War, the Cold War had begun. Brecht managed to be cleverly evasive about his political convictions and stated, truthfully, that he had never been a member of any party.

His first stay back in Europe was in Switzerland, but then he and Helene Weigel went on to Berlin, in the communist part (the Soviet sector) of post-war divided Germany. The German Democratic Republic provided Brecht and Weigel with their own theatre: in 1949 Brecht's 'Berlin Ensemble' presented their first production (of *Mother Courage*) in their own space. Much of Brecht's time and energy over the next years were devoted to running the theatre and working with actors on productions. On 10 August 1956, aged fifty-eight, Brecht died of a heart attack.

Origins and writing of the play

Brecht used two main sources as inspiration for *The Caucasian Chalk Circle*. In the 1920s he read a German translation of an old Chinese play, *The Circle of Chalk*, in which an emperor's main wife tries to claim another wife's child as her own. A wise judge orders them to pull the child across a chalk line. The biological mother, not wanting to hurt the child, lets him go and the judge recognizes her as the true mother. Brecht was also familiar with the biblical story of King Solomon (1 Kings 3:16–28), who decided a similar case by proposing to cut the child in two with a sword; the true mother would rather give up her child than see him killed and she is therefore awarded the child. Apart from this central motif, everything else in the play – the setting, the characters, the figure of Azdak as judge and his other cases – is Brecht's invention.

Brecht worked on *The Caucasian Chalk Circle* during his years in exile. In 1940, while in Sweden, he wrote a short story called 'The Augsburg Chalk Circle' which already presents most of the plot – the desertion and adoption, the court case with the test and its outcome – and is set in Germany in the seventeenth century during the Thirty Years War. In April and May 1944, during the Second World War, while he was living in California, he wrote most of the play and also decided on the Caucasus as the setting, which is in Grusinia (Georgia), then part of the Soviet Union (since 1921 and until the dissolution of the USSR in 1991, when Georgia declared its independence). At this time, Brecht shared the optimism of many that the communist regime in the Soviet Union was building a better society, with more justice and new ways of organizing property collectively and using it for the benefit of all. He was hoping that the Soviet Union, with its socialist politics, would be a progressive power helping reconstruction after the defeat of the Germans, which is why we have a 'Reconstruction Commission' in the Prologue of the play.

Brecht revised the play in 1948–9, after the end of the war, and it had its premiere at Carleton College in Minnesota, USA. This is the version of the play you are reading. In 1953–4 Brecht reworked the play again and had composer Paul Dessau write music for it. In 1954 the play was performed for the first time in German, in Brecht's theatre in East Berlin.

Synopsis

Prologue
Very shortly after the end of the Second World War in the Caucasus, members of two agricultural collectives debate the future of what used to be the land of a goat farm. It had been abandoned because the German army took over the area. The members of the former goat farm would like to return and resume their work, but members of a neighbouring fruit farm would like to use the area, which they consider very suitable for orchards and vineyards. A delegate from the government oversees the discussion, which proceeds peacefully and ends with an agreement that the new plans by the fruit growers promise the best use of the land. In honour of the guests, a famous singer has been asked to perform, joined by members of the fruit collective. It is this performance, 'The Chalk Circle', that we see in the following five scenes. (In other words, in what follows, *The Caucasian Chalk Circle* refers to Brecht's play as a whole, whereas 'The Chalk Circle' refers to the play-within-the-play, that is, Scenes 1–5.)

Pages 7–12

Scene 1: The Noble Child
The Singer introduces the situation and characters, taking us back to a past age in Grusinia. We see the Governor, Georgi Abashwili, his wife, Natella, and their baby son, Michael, on

Pages 13–29

Easter Sunday, surrounded by crowds and accompanied by soldiers and two doctors. The Fat Prince, Arsen Kazbeki, greets the Governor and his family. The Governor is preoccupied with his plans for expanding his palace and garden, while his wife is concerned about their precious son's health. The Governor refuses to hear an urgent messenger who has arrived from the capital before church.

One of the palace guards, Simon Shashava, greets Grusha Vashnadze, a kitchen maid, and flirts with her somewhat clumsily.

The Fat Prince signals secretly to the palace guards of the Governor, who defers hearing the messenger once again. It turns out that the Prince and the palace guards, the Ironshirts, have conspired to overthrow the Governor as part of a rebellion of the Princes against the Governors and the Grand Duke.

The Governor is subsequently taken prisoner, the servants rush about, the two doctors quarrel. Grusha chides Simon for his foolish loyalty to the Governor. Simon asks Grusha a series of questions leading up to a marriage proposal, which Grusha accepts without delay.

The Governor's wife is obsessed with packing up as many of her expensive clothes as she can. Eventually she realizes the danger she is in. In her haste to escape she abandons her baby, who is handed over to Grusha by one of Natella's maids before she flees herself. Grusha's fellow servants warn her about the danger she is putting herself in and she reluctantly decides she must leave Michael behind. The Fat Prince has arranged the assassination of the Governor; now he is looking for the child but fails to find him. Grusha is stopped from leaving by the Singer's song in the name of the child. She ends up changing her mind and decides to take him along.

Scene 2: The Flight into the Northern Mountains

Grusha is on her way to the Northern Mountains with a hungry Michael and not enough money to feed him, since the war has made even milk much more expensive. Meanwhile, two of the Ironshirts, who are now under the command of the Fat Prince, are pursuing her.

Pages 30–43

Grusha reluctantly leaves Michael at the door of a farmhouse, persuading herself that he will find a good home there. She waits until she sees the farmer's wife taking him in, but as she walks on she runs into the Ironshirts, who speak to her roughly and lewdly, asking about Michael. Grusha hurries back to the farmhouse, where she tries to persuade the farmer's wife not to give away Michael's identity, but the farmwoman's resolve fails when the soldiers catch up with Grusha. As the Ironshirts realize they have found the precious heir, Grusha strikes down the higher-ranking one of the two and flees with Michael.

Having thus thrown her fate in with the child's, Grusha makes the decision to adopt him. With the Ironshirts in pursuit, she risks the precarious crossing over a dangerously decayed bridge with him rather than leave him behind.

Scene 3: In the Northern Mountains

Carrying Michael, Grusha arrives at the house of her married brother, Lavrenti, in a state of near-total exhaustion. Her sister-in-law, Aniko, interrogates her with little regard for Grusha's state, except to worry about catching a disease from her. Her brother quickly confers with Grusha about the child to make up a cover story that will appease his wife.

Pages 44–62

After Grusha has spent the winter with the reluctant couple, spring comes and her brother urges her to leave. Realizing that she has no place to go, he has come up with a plan. He proposes marrying Grusha to a dying peasant in a different village, which will legitimize her child in the eyes of others but not commit her to an actual marriage. He has secretly taken some of his wife's money to finance this scheme.

Grusha and her brother arrive at the house of the bridegroom, Jussup, and his mother. The bridegroom appears to be close to death; the mother is mainly concerned with money and accepts another 200 piasters to turn a blind eye to Grusha's child. Neighbours arrive before she returns with the drunk monk whom she has hired on the cheap to officiate at the wedding. A ceremony is performed hurriedly. The monk has invited his musician friends – more mouths to feed, in the eyes of the mother, who is worried about having enough cakes for the guests. The guests discuss the husband's state of health along with news of the war, and their suspicion that he faked his illness to escape military service. They reveal that the war has ended. Grusha, realizing that this means Simon is coming back, starts praying. Suddenly Jussup, who has been listening, rises up, scaring his guests and telling them to leave.

Both Grusha and Jussup are unhappy. Grusha is stuck in her arranged marriage and tries her best to avoid any physical intimacy with him, while he vents his frustration with her and the situation he finds himself in.

Time passes and Michael has grown. He is playing with the older children while Grusha watches him as she washes linen in the river. Simon Shashava arrives and Grusha and he exchange greetings. Simon has advanced in rank and been given a pay rise. Grusha's attempts to explain her vexed situation confuse him and cause him to think that she is no longer committed to him. At the very moment when she tries to tell him that Michael is not her child, Ironshirts show up and take

Synopsis   11

the boy into custody as the presumed son of the late Governor and his wife. Grusha's loyalty to Michael makes her claim him, at which point Simon leaves. The Singer informs us that the competing claims on the child – Grusha's and Natella Abashwili's – will be settled by trial in the court of a judge named Azdak.

Scene 4: The Story of the Judge
This scene shifts us back in time to the beginning of the revolution we saw in Scene 2 and introduces the second main character of the play, the village scribe Azdak. A disreputable-looking Azdak provides shelter and food for an old man whom he takes for a beggar. When he realizes that his guest is a nobleman, he decides to throw him out, but is interrupted by the arrival of the village policeman, Shauwa, who begs Azdak not to poach rabbits. Azdak decides not to deliver the fugitive into his hands.

Pages 63–85

When Azdak discovers that he has sheltered the Grand Duke himself, he forces Shauwa to take him to the city of Nuka, where he theatrically denounces himself for harbouring the Grand Duke and demands a trial and punishment from the assembled Ironshirts in the courthouse. He refers to the war in Persia and the revolution that followed under the impression that a similar revolution, one driven by the people, has done away with the ruling classes in Grusinia. But the Ironshirts, it turns out, have not only hanged the judge; they are also crushing the rebellious working classes, and Azdak quickly distances himself from the position he had so proudly proclaimed.

The Fat Prince arrives and proposes his nephew as the new judge. With the Grand Duke (thanks to Azdak) still at large, the Princes feel less than secure in their new-found power and the Ironshirts realize that the Princes need their support. The

Ironshirts ask Azdak how he feels about the nephew for judge and Azdak proposes a mock trial to test the Fat Prince's nephew, offering himself as fake defendant and assuming the role of the Grand Duke. Azdak, mimicking the Grand Duke's clipped language, defends himself against the charge of having lost the war by implicating the Princes, whose profiteering, he claims, lost the war. His spirited performance entertains and impresses the Ironshirts, who send away the nephew and declare the 'rascal' Azdak as judge.

Azdak remains in the position of judge for two years, and the scene continues with three of his cases. In the first, Azdak actually combines two cases — one between a doctor and his patient, the other against a blackmailer. Azdak causes mayhem with his verdicts and defies expectations of justice while offering hilariously cynical pronouncements on the lucrative practice of medicine. The case also shows us that Azdak is happy to solicit bribes and accept money.

The second trial concerns charges brought by an innkeeper against his stable-hand, who allegedly molested the farmer's daughter-in-law Ludovica in her husband's absence. Azdak extracts a bribe from him, but the innkeeper ignores the additional interest that Azdak expresses in the innkeeper's horse. After interviewing the voluptuous and naïve Ludovica, whose statement sounds suspiciously well rehearsed, Azdak declares the culprit not to be the stable-hand but Ludovica for seducing him, and then goes off to the stable with her.

In the final case, Azdak hears a complaint brought by three rich farmers against a poor peasant woman, whose brother-in-law, the bandit Irakli, has stolen from them to support her. The woman defends herself by claiming she received the stolen goods through a miracle. When the bandit shows up at the tavern where court is held and claims to be a wandering hermit, Azdak welcomes him warmly. In her testimony, the peasant woman portrays Irakli as a saintly figure. Far from intimidating and beating up the farmers and their servants, in her account Irakli transforms them into generous donors. Azdak happily accepts her version of events. Rather than return their property to the rich farmers, he fines them for not believing in miracles.

After Azdak has dispensed this kind of justice for two years, the situation reverts to pre-revolutionary conditions with the return of the Grand Duke from exile in Persia, the reappearance of the Governor's wife and renewed social unrest. The Fat Prince, instigator of the revolution, has been killed. Azdak realizes that his solidarity with the poor against the wealthy has made him notorious and vulnerable to retaliation now that the previous rulers are in power again. He is scared and acts in a cowardly and submissive manner towards the Governor's wife, who approaches him in preparation for her petition in court to have Michael returned to her.

Scene 5: The Chalk Circle

Against a background of signs that indicate the disorders continue (distant noises, fire, soldiers), the trial begins. Grusha tries to explain to the Governor's former cook, her friend and ally, why she is not willing to give up Michael. The cook thinks Grusha may have a chance with Azdak as judge, especially if he is drunk. Both she and Simon are willing to lie for Grusha. Simon exchanges a brief greeting with her. Grusha has a close encounter with the Ironshirt corporal she almost killed when she rescued Michael.

The Governor's wife appears, accompanied by the Adjutant and two lawyers, who warn her not to speak negatively of the common people. They expect that a new judge will replace Azdak at the command of the Grand Duke. Azdak has been

Pages 86–99

denounced by the three farmers against whom he ruled and now is physically abused by the Ironshirts. They are getting ready to hang him when a messenger arrives from the Grand Duke, who, it turns out, is reappointing Azdak. Azdak recovers sufficiently to take the judge's chair and opens court as he usually does, by accepting bribes – in this case, from the lawyers of the Governor's wife. Her lawyers offer an eloquent plea for the child. Azdak turns to Grusha, whose answer is direct and simple: she speaks of how she brought up Michael. The second lawyer admits that the Governor's wife – and they – want the child because only Michael will give her access to the Governor's land and money. Azdak now turns to Grusha and questions her and her allies, accusing her, the cook and Simon of lying. He appears annoyed at not receiving any money from Grusha and gets sidetracked into engaging in a contest of folk idioms with Simon. Azdak starts fining Grusha's party and further provokes Grusha until she expresses her low opinion of him without restraint. Azdak seems to listen with approval; then he suddenly switches briefly to a different case and queries an old married couple who are seeking a divorce. When he turns to Grusha and questions her again – why wouldn't she want the boy to have the advantages of wealth? – the Singer expresses Grusha's silent thoughts. The two competing women engage in an argument, which Azdak stops by announcing that since the case cannot be decided on the evidence, he has devised a test to identify the true mother. He places the child in a circle drawn with chalk on the floor and claims that whichever woman it is will be able to muster more strength and pull him to her side. The women pull twice and both times Grusha lets go, not wanting to hurt the child she has raised.

Based on the evidence of her behaviour, Azdak declares Grusha to be the mother and confiscates the land of the Governor's wife for the use of all children. Before he steps down as judge, he absent-mindedly signs a divorce decree: as it turns out, he has divorced not the old couple but Grusha and Jussup. Simon happily pays their fines to the judge and they all dance. Azdak disappears and is never seen again, but he is remembered fondly. The Singer's final lines return us to the Prologue, as he reminds everyone that 'what there is shall go to those who are good for it'.

Scene-by-Scene Analysis and Commentary

Prologue

Two positions – old and new

Note that the Prologue has a specific date: it is set in the summer of 1945, right after the end of the devastating Second World War. The Germans have just been defeated by the Allies – Britain, the USA, France and the Soviet Union – and the Caucasus was one of the places where the war raged. Brecht is specific in using elements of communist life in the Soviet Union: farming is organized in the form of 'collectives' and not based on individual property, and the characters in the Prologue mostly do not use names or titles, but address one another as 'Comrade', showing solidarity and equality.

The Prologue is also called 'The Dispute about the Valley'. The Delegate, a state official, outlines a conflict between the previous inhabitants of the valley, the goat farmers, who were forced to leave because of the war, and the new group, who propose a fruit farm.

This is a clear conflict of interests, but it is handled in an unexpected way, and several things point us to the manner in which the dispute is conducted. First, at the beginning all participants are sitting in a circle, not in two opposed groups. In fact, sometimes it is difficult to tell who is on which side, especially when members of both groups remember the war they jointly fought against the outside enemy. They are drinking and

Pages 7–10

smoking together – signs of a peaceful gathering. And they consider this discussion a 'pleasure', along with tobacco and wine. Also, the Delegate is not making a decision. Instead, he asks the two groups to decide together, placing the matter in their hands.

The Old Man, a member of the dairy collective, starts out with an unconventional approach: he presents not a verbal argument but a cheese for everyone to share. The cheese is sampled by all and we should assume that it is excellent. But the Old Man explains that it is not as good as it should be since the goats do not like their new grazing grounds. His arguments are strongly inflected by a wish to return to how things used to be. Several others join him in arguments that are more emotional than rational. These are not rejected out of hand: the Delegate acknowledges that love for one's land is a valid point. But members of the fruit collective point out that there must be scope for development and that land is also a tool for all. The important point made is that times change and even laws may have to change to fit changing circumstances.

A peaceful resolution – and art to celebrate it

Pages 10–12 Kato makes a good case for why the fruit farm needs the additional land. He emphasizes that planning it was quite a challenge during the war and we can see how both groups are warmly united in remembering their joint fight against fascism. Solidarity and reason are shown to prevail over conflicting interests.

The discussion turns technical and the planning details for the fruit farm convince the dairy farmers to give up their rights – amid more friendly banter. (From today's perspective we might well question the 'bigger-is-better' logic of the new project and the impact it will have on the valley, and the uncritical belief that technology and construction provide the way to a better future. But remember that the play was written in the 1940s and reflects the technological optimism of that time.) It is clear that everyone enjoys the discussion and camaraderie, even though much is at stake and the outcome will have a considerable impact on everyone's future. The tone is relaxed and humorous, and the 'dispute' concludes with a performance organized by the fruit farmers in honour of the dairy collective.

We are shown that scientific facts and engineering blueprints, along with sentimental thoughts and emotions, all have their place in this enlightened society that has moved beyond self-interest. Finally, the Prologue makes a statement about art as an essential component. The fruit growers, having gained the valley, invite their guests to a celebration with the well-known Singer, Arkadi Tscheidse, who knows the old songs. Will they fit a changed society? The Singer insists that 'old poetry can sound well in the shadow of new tractors' (p. 12), that old wisdom and new can be combined harmoniously. Much of the Prologue is about combining the best of the old with the best of the new. The Delegate is shown to be too one-sided in his thinking, valuing economics more than art. He would like the play to be shorter, but the Singer's curt 'no' to his request makes it very clear that art needs its time and must not be considered less relevant than more practical concerns.

The five scenes that follow constitute the 'old legend' of the Chalk Circle performed by the Singer and his four musicians. A number of actors are needed as well as a Chorus – in most stagings, the peasants and tractorists now put on costumes and act the roles of the characters in the 'Chinese' play that follows. The Prologue is sometimes omitted in staging Brecht's *Caucasian Chalk Circle* (in other words, what is performed is the 'Chalk Circle' play of Scenes 1–5 only), but Brecht himself considered it essential for what he wanted to say about human nature and human society.

Important elements of this scene

The Prologue ties a play set in an unspecified past to the present in which it was written. It presents a harmonious, democratic, cooperative and rational way of decision-making. The dispute does not pit two factions against each other, but – ignoring their competing claims – unites them in one circle as they work together to decide on the most beneficial solution. Realistically, the majority of conflicts will never be solved quite this peacefully. What we see is an ideal towards which Brecht felt humans should be working. The world shaped according to this ideal harmoniously combines old and new knowledge and laws, emotions and rational-technical arguments, and art is taken just as seriously as economics and science. Finally, the Prologue provides a frame for all that follows, which is presented as a play performed under the direction of the Singer by and for the characters in the Prologue.

Scene 1: The Noble Child

Rulers in feudal times

Pages 13–16   The Singer simultaneously directs the small group of performers. He knows his text largely by heart and the 'well-thumbed' book shows that the play is an often-performed classic.

He now provides an introduction and setting for the play in a song that presents Governor Abashwili and his wife, Natella, to us. His song already contains important elements that help us assess the situation. It mentions that the old times we are about to witness were 'bloody'. The Governor has wealth and power in the form of horses and soldiers – but many of his subjects live in poverty, and the soldiers are needed to protect him from the beggars and petitioners. The luxury in which he and his family live is contrasted with the dissatisfaction of the people under him, for whom life appears to be hard. There are so many people in need of help that they crowd around him, preventing his progress. While soldiers pass out money as charity, others dispense violence, keeping the crowd at bay with whips: the Governor is protected from too much direct contact with his subjects. There are several mentions of the war the Governor is waging in Persia, in which his subjects fight and suffer. Slums will have to make way for his new garden, with no thought for where the displaced inhabitants are going to live. Yet his subjects admire the Governor and the new baby.

The Fat Prince makes a show of exaggerated and insincere cheerfulness when talking with the Governor and his wife. Natella Abashwili reacts hysterically to a cough from the baby, which leads to a display of concern from the two doctors. But their concern is really for their own position – their safety and their pay – not for the baby. Under a thin veneer of politeness the two doctors are bitter rivals locked in poisonous competition. Note the way in which one of the doctors is made out to be a slave to authority. Even when recommending the temperature of the child's bath water – a most common-sensical decision – he feels the need to cite a medical expert.

The Governor, it appears, is happier to show himself to the people in a splendid ceremonial procession and enjoy his Sunday than to attend to politics. The arrival of a wounded, dust-covered messenger from the capital should have signalled trouble, but the Governor defers reading his urgent papers. Before entering the church, he also leaves us with a question: if the Fat Prince is speaking of rain, where was he last night (p. 16)?

Kitchen maid and soldier – the working class

Pages 16–18   As Simon Shashava, the guard, strikes up a conversation with kitchen maid Grusha Vashnadze, we realize he is interested in her. He reveals that he has watched her doing the laundry in the river, baring her leg as she did so. Grusha is annoyed, especially at the thought that he might have played the voyeur in the company of other soldiers. We see that Grusha is conscientious, hard-working, simple and direct. Simon, finding himself in hot water in his attempt to flirt with her, hastily tries to reassure her that he did not bring along a friend. Later we will see that his interest in her is genuine, and that Grusha reciprocates it. Both address one another mostly in the third person ('the young lady', 'the soldier'), which gives their exchange a formal and old-fashioned air.

A rebellion

Pages 18–21   The Singer starts us out with questions that expressly recall the subtly disturbing signs we may already have noticed: his folk-ballad-like song expresses the fact that the Governor's time has run out and anticipates what we are about to see performed.

As always, stage directions (in italics) can provide important cues here. We see (p. 18) that the Fat Prince has some kind of understanding with the Ironshirts and gives them a signal before the Governor and his family return from church. It is made even clearer that the Governor lives a life of luxury and that his wife is jealous of little Michael, who is more important to him than she is. Next, in a nice bit of irony, the Governor's Adjutant reassures the architects that there is nothing to worry about politically and emphasizes the loyalty of the local soldiers precisely at the moment they turn on the Governor. One of the architects explains that the Princes have been plotting against the Grand Duke and his Governors (so now we know where the Fat Prince encountered rain the night before).

The Singer comments on the way those in power always seem to assume that their power will last for ever, even though it is built on oppressing the people. The praise of change and hope in his song returns to the necessity for change already brought up in the Prologue.

The Governor is brought out in chains and the Singer addresses him directly. Now he initiates a shift in perspective for us in the images he uses: all convey the idea that the working people often suffer along with the great when they fall, even though they did not derive any advantages from their superiors' reign while they were in power. With this, we turn to the panicked servants. The two doctors appear: we realize that they have no sense of medical responsibility and obligation to their employers. They were paid servants and now, without any qualms, leave the Governor's wife and her precious son, who has become nothing but a 'little brat' to them.

Grusha and Simon: a marriage proposal in turbulent times

Simon comes looking for Grusha, who is thinking of escaping and seeking refuge with her brother. It turns out that Simon is one of the soldiers who is planning to remain loyal and accompany the Governor's wife to safety. While we may admire him for his soldierly sense of duty, Grusha displays common sense and an awareness of class differences. She tries to reason with him and tells him plainly that he is stupid to risk his own life for someone who means nothing to him. Simon comes to the heart of the matter and starts to ask personal questions about Grusha, again in the formal third person. Simon's questions – about Grusha's family, her health and her character – while probably appearing less than romantic to us, are part of a

Pages 21–3

traditional courtship and betrothal. We are also getting to know Simon, who is deliberate and systematic rather than quick-witted. He has confidence in his own judgement, thinks before he speaks and stands behind every sentence he utters. He likes side comments and typically speaks in folk idioms and proverbs. Grusha is faster at getting to the point. After reiterating that a man should not risk his life unnecessarily, she tries to cut short his somewhat ponderous speech and in fact accepts his proposal before he can finish making it (here Brecht offers a comic accent in a serious scene). Nudged out of his deliberate pace, Simon is pleased that Grusha has found out the region where he is from. The fact that she wanted this information signals that she has also been interested in him.

This is not a melodramatic, highly emotional scene of the kind we would see in a Hollywood film. Brecht wants things to slow down here, so that while revolution rages around them, these two characters, very plainly and simply, declare their allegiance to one another, with Simon's silver cross in place of an engagement ring. Here, as in many other instances, Brecht uses contradictions: he emphasizes their closeness with the ceremonial distance between them. Furthermore, Brecht gives Grusha the time to sing a beautiful song for Simon, assuring him that she will wait for him (p. 23). Only after they have bowed to one another (no kisses here – everything displays the formality of ancient tradition) does the pace pick up again.

A child is left behind and rescued

Pages 23–9 From Grusha and Simon's level-headed behaviour, their directness and the simple dignity of their engagement, we move to the Governor's wife, Natella Abashwili. Brecht stages a dramatic contrast here. As the Adjutant tries desperately to hurry her along, she displays more of her true character, behaving in contrast to her prior composure with Simon and Grusha.

Scene-by-Scene Analysis and Commentary

Surrounded by her possessions, she tries to decide which of her fancy dresses she cannot do without, while berating her servants and voicing petty criticisms. Note her language: her speech is almost entirely made up of complaints and orders. We begin to feel not only that she is foolish not to recognize the danger she is in but also that the trappings of luxury are the only thing she cares about. And indeed, as the Adjutant finally manages to hustle her away, Michael, supposedly the apple of her eye, is left behind. He is given to Grusha to hold when his nursemaid runs off as well. As the other maids hurry to save themselves, they try to persuade Grusha to leave the baby and go with them. She decides to leave the child after wrapping him up solicitously, waiting until the soldiers and the Fat Prince are out of the way.

The Fat Prince oversees the mounting of the Governor's severed head on the wall. As Grusha gets ready to leave, she catches sight of the gruesome head, which emphasizes the danger she is in and the ruthlessness of the Fat Prince and his Ironshirts. But in spite of the danger, she pauses, and the Singer provides us with insight into her thoughts and emotions in the final – and important – song of the scene. She imagines the child calling out to her, which makes good sense, but instead of appearing to be begging for her help, the child asks calmly for it, and his following words are surprising as well. He reasons with her, explaining what it would mean not to him but to *her* if she left him here. Closing her heart to his plight would not allow her to experience other gentle and positive emotions in her life subsequently, and would mar her enjoyment of love, nature and the community with others. This call to be human and help another person in need appeals to Grusha and she hesitates again to leave the child. Even though she knows she should go, she forms an attachment to the child.

Brecht also wants us to ask whether Grusha is not acting

just the way she told Simon not to act, putting his life in danger. But Simon was doing so for a stupid, spoilt woman, while Grusha sees a small innocent child. There is a moral here: one cannot be helpful only when it is convenient and risk-free. Finally, Grusha gives way to her human decency and, against her better reason ('sighing' as she picks up the child), she takes Michael along. The Singer intones, 'Fearful is the seductive power of goodness!' (p. 29) – as though goodness were a sign of weakness. We all know that doing good is preferable, but Brecht wants us to see how complicated things can get, and to understand that decisions are rarely clear cut. Saving Michael, Grusha puts herself on the wrong side of the new law of the revolution, and she knows it.

Important elements of this scene

The first scene establishes a past feudal situation where the peasants are oppressed by the Governor and where rivalry between those in power leads to a revolution by the Princes against the Grand Duke and his Governors. Among a number of characters, it introduces us to Grusha, whom we will follow throughout the play. Brecht's message in portraying the Governor and his wife is that power and status corrupt people. Brecht shows them as ignorant, arrogant and deeply unlikeable. Brecht sets up Simon and Grusha's relationship in a quietly beautiful engagement scene, in contrast to the chaotic revolution that unfolds around them. He shows them exercising their common sense as thoughtful, simple people whose hearts are in the right place and who compare very favourably with spoilt, unpleasant rulers.

The Governor and his wife have no apparent redeeming qualities. Brecht establishes the Governor's wife as a careless and irresponsible mother. Against her negative example, he sets up Grusha, who is moved by common decency and acts

Scene-by-Scene Analysis and Commentary

against her own self-interest. Reluctantly, she decides to take care of the abandoned baby, whose life is in danger not only because his mother and the other servants have deserted him but also because he is a pawn in the power struggle of the revolution.

The revolution, Simon and Grusha's engagement and Grusha's decision not to walk away from the child are the three main events that set the plot in motion. The Singer's remark about the seductive power of goodness can be read as a general question: What is the state of the world if doing good, and doing the right thing, carry so much risk?

Scene 2: The Flight into the Northern Mountains

Expensive milk

Again, the Singer – joined by the Chorus – introduces the scene. His words sound innocuous, even boring, and deliberately undramatic: Grusha will sing a song and buy milk. But we will see that buying milk is not as simple as it sounds; and the Chorus tells us what is at stake, reminding us that soldiers – 'bloodhounds' – are in pursuit of the Governor's baby.

Pages 30–32

We see Grusha singing an upbeat and humorous folk song about four generals who went to Persia, all of whom turn out to be incompetent. It is a man of the people who succeeds and is able to fight the war as it should be fought.

Grusha stops to buy milk for the baby from an old man, but it turns out to be almost beyond her means. Brecht wanted the price of the milk to be about a week of Grusha's wages, so she would have to spend a lot of her precious money on it. She offers the baby her milkless breast, but realizes she will have to buy him nourishment after all. She complains about the old man and feels that he is taking advantage of her situation.

Pursuit by the Ironshirts and an adoption

Pages 32–9 We see two Ironshirts, who have been sent to find and retrieve the baby since he threatens the success of the Princes, who have taken power. The slightly higher-ranking one, a Corporal, berates his subordinate for being insufficiently soldierly and not embracing violence, unthinking obedience and death. The Corporal is clearly more cruel than his fellow soldier, but both embody brutality and stupidity.

The Singer tells us that keeping Michael is too hard for Grusha. We see Grusha outside a farmhouse. The peasant woman is well nourished and there is obviously plenty of milk to be had. So Grusha puts Michael down and tries to convince him – or rather, herself – that she must leave him. Her reasons are both practical and emotional. She has no nappies, we have seen that milk is too expensive for her, she is probably exhausted and she is thinking of her future with Simon.

When the peasant woman discovers Michael, she is surprised first by him and then by his fine linen. Perhaps she appreciates it, perhaps she is suspicious of it, since this is a time when luxury and being from a noble family point to danger. She laments the upheavals they are experiencing. Michael wakes up and she quickly bonds with him. Her husband is thinking about the cost of feeding a baby – in fact, Brecht wanted him to complain about another mouth while eating from his soup bowl. But his wife plays down the importance of the cost. Ignoring her husband's protests, she decides they will take the baby in.

Having made sure he will be safe, Grusha leaves Michael with mixed feelings, which the Singer expresses in a way that brings out their contradictory nature: sad at being free, she is cheerful at having been replaced. But soon she runs into the Ironshirts. The Corporal approaches her with sexually suggestive wordplay and double-talk that show him relishing his power over her. His claim (p. 35) that Simon had given him the key to look in on Grusha recalls the soldiers' song earlier ('My friends will keep her honour safe', p. 33), but it sounds much more like a threat. When Grusha realizes they are looking for Michael, she runs and – with brief comments by the Singer and Chorus – stumbles into the farmhouse, where she gives the peasant woman a breathless summary. The peasant woman puts on an air of strength and determination, but crumbles when she hears of the danger. Grusha quickly tries to instil courage in her and provides some coaching, showing her own strength and resourcefulness. Only when she appeals to the peasant woman in her identity as a mother does the strategy seem to work.

The Ironshirts enter, and the Corporal continues his lewd remarks towards Grusha. We can tell he is attracted to her: in fact, he is trying to get the peasant woman out of the house, probably in preparation to make a move on Grusha. He is perfectly willing to exploit his power, and his thoughts are not at all on his task or on the baby. But the peasant woman is understandably afraid. Too panicked to realize that she is in no immediate danger, she blurts out the truth to him, dooming Michael. In order to save him, Grusha commits an unplanned and desperate act of violence against the Corporal.

After twenty-two days of flight with Michael, Grusha decides to adopt him. Interestingly, in her song she phrases this as a *mutual* adoption – for want of a better alternative for either of them, they are stuck with each other. We can see that Michael is in good hands and that he can truly rely on her.

Grusha's words are characteristically unsentimental and plain as she assures him (and us) that they will stay together. In a symbolic act of severance from his past, she throws away his fine linen.

A narrow escape

Pages 39–43 Grusha's resolve is put to the test soon after, when she comes to a broken bridge. Grusha is in considerable danger. She could save herself much more easily if she left Michael behind. Instead, she risks her life for him. The exchange with the three merchants serves to reinforce the urgency and desperate nature of the situation – and yet Brecht has Grusha pause and sing a little song of resolve to Michael, telling him she accepts the danger and suffering that they will have to face together.

Grusha bravely makes it to the other side and the merchants keep off the Ironshirts, even though the woman among them also criticizes her. Grusha walks on, offering Michael consoling words about the wind and snow that make them out to be fellow members of the working class, and useful ones, rather than his enemies. She sings a song that 'revises' his family lineage, as a way of telling him about the bright future she sees opening up for him as he escapes his origins and the social class he was born into. In spite of their status as members of the elite (or perhaps because of it, Brecht might want to say), his father acted like a bandit and his mother like a harlot. In contrast, Michael will be honourable – and honoured by others – because Grusha will bring him up to be a decent person.

Important elements of this scene

This scene reinforces our positive impression of Grusha. A whole series of events end up testing the bond between Grusha and Michael, showing us that Grusha does not run away from difficulties but faces them and acts decisively when necessary. Scene 2 also offers us some of Brecht's typical attention to detail – the exchange of milk for money, the peasant woman's response to the fine linen, Grusha's attempt to help the peasant woman find courage in her own authority as a mother. It also shows us two strong and decisive women – though Grusha more so than the peasant woman, whose resolve fails in the face of direct confrontation with the Ironshirts. The Ironshirts are villains who play a small but necessary role throughout all five scenes. Even though they are minor figures, we find Brecht in this scene delineating their unpleasant character in brief but telling detail, mostly through the language used. This scene is permeated by war and we see the way it affects all the characters' lives. Its end affirms Grusha's decision to adopt Michael as her own.

Scene 3: In the Northern Mountains

Family ties and their limits

The Singer tells us that for seven more days Grusha walked through ice and cold and endured much hardship, and she looks forward to the reunion with her now-married brother and the support she expects he will offer her. Her hopes are quite reasonable, but the Singer is setting both her and the audience up for a disappointment. Her brother, Lavrenti, greets her with astonishment rather than warmth, and her sister-in-law, Aniko, subjects her to a number of critical questions while continuing to order her servants around.

Pages 44–7

The stage directions tell an important part of the story and highlight the contrast between the characters: Grusha is utterly exhausted and no doubt starving, and is met with coldness and suspicion. We must imagine these narrow-minded farmers, set-in-their-ways in a remote place where everyone knows each other and few visitors pass through. While the well-fed couple sit down to a rich meal, they offer Grusha neither food nor even a seat. It becomes clear quickly that Lavrenti defers to his wife (in contrast, we saw a peasant couple in the previous scene where the wife made the decisions). The Singer makes the point that Lavrenti came into the farm and its prosperity by marriage, meaning that he has little say in the running of things. He is mainly concerned with what she will think about Grusha's situation. When he calls his wife 'religious', we quickly understand that he means it in the sense of 'rigidly moral', not of someone who acts kindly and unselfishly towards others – not even family members.

As Grusha collapses from exhaustion and hunger, Aniko keeps worrying about catching a disease from her, meanwhile urging her husband to eat his meat (a luxury) and deliberately leaving Grusha unfed. She goes on interrogating Grusha, while Lavrenti tries to mediate and improvises some answers intended to make his wife feel a little more merciful. His claim that she 'has a good heart' – if only after supper! – is clearly contradicted by the facts at hand. Perhaps he is deceiving himself or just wants to cover for her failure to show even the most basic kindness towards Grusha. Although he is not actively unkind himself, he has been shaped by his decision to marry a woman with property, and he is clearly a coward, as the Singer will also state.

An unwelcome suggestion of marriage for Grusha

Pages 47–9 Time passes. The Singer's words tell us that Lavrenti and his wife took Grusha in only very reluctantly. The winter was long because it was dark and cold – but it was simultaneously short because Lavrenti and Aniko will want to get rid of their unwelcome guests as soon as spring comes. Grusha knows she will have to leave, but does not know where to go with Michael.

Scene-by-Scene Analysis and Commentary 33

Thus she awaits spring with anxiety. We see her sitting in a very cold room, where she is at work weaving. Her thoughts are obviously with Simon as she sings a song. Just as she warned him not to act with foolish courage, so too does the girl in the song tell her betrothed not to go to the front or the back of the army, but to stay in the centre, where the chances of survival are best. Her song also teachers Michael how to stay alive. She herself is surviving by making no demands, not complaining, trying to be inconspicuous. Acting like cockroaches might sound unheroic, but it is a way to survive.

Lavrenti enters and the conversation between him and Grusha is full of unspoken tension. Lavrenti expresses apparent concern for her, asking if it is too cold or if there are rats. But his meaning is the opposite, as Grusha well knows, and he is only looking for excuses to make her leave. She attempts to counter his attempts – by taking off her shawl and not complaining about the cold, by pretending the melting snow is a leaking barrel. Lavrenti's hypocrisy is apparent in the way he inserts markers of time ('You've been here six months, haven't you?' 'When d'you think he'll come?'), questions her about her 'soldier-husband' and tries to portray his wife as a sensitive soul full of worries about Grusha – all inconsistent with the narrow-minded and selfish character we have seen. The dripping of melting snow accompanies the one-sided conversation like a timer that is running out and accelerating in the process: it marks the mounting tension and inserts pressure into all the insincere questions.

Lavrenti finally comes out with it: it is spring, people are talking about Grusha's child and she needs to leave. But he does care for his sister even if he cannot stand up to his wife, and he has concocted a plan: he has found her a husband. When Grusha protests – after all, she is engaged to Simon – he replies that his solution is perfect, since it will make her not a wife but a widow: 'You don't need a man in bed – you need a man on paper. And I've found you one. The son of this peasant woman is going to die. Isn't that wonderful?' (Brecht frequently makes us realize that almost everything is a matter of perspective. He does so here with the jolting and unfeeling 'Isn't that wonderful?' when referring to a man on his death bed.) From both Grusha's and Lavrenti's perspectives, the man's sad state is indeed wonderful given what they need, even though Lavrenti's joy sounds a little macabre. Grusha realizes, of course, that this must be a financial transaction in essence, and Lavrenti admits to stealing from his wife to make this happen – an act that is simultaneously courageous in its solidarity with Grusha, and cowardly, since it is done in secret and involves a plan to appease his wife's self-righteous piety.

Grusha seems to chide Michael for the trouble he has brought her and she calls herself a fool for picking him up in the first place. Here it is up to the director how he or she wants to play the scene. Grusha could say the words with tender affection, which would be more like 'regular' traditional theatre; or she could utter them drily, factually – Michael is used to her practical thinking, and in practical terms she is right. As we will see, her sacrifices for Michael will only increase.

An unwanted husband and an odd wedding

Pages 49–56 The Singer sums up the situation before the wedding succinctly in three lines and then tells us that Lavrenti will hide the child during the wedding. Clearly, he had kept Michael's existence a secret from Grusha's future mother-in-law during negotiations. The mother is clearly eager for money – whether because she is greedy or merely desperately poor. It appears that her main emotion thinking about her son's death is to make sure the wedding can still take place so that she will receive her payment. She talks about her shame at seeing Michael, but is

Scene-by-Scene Analysis and Commentary 35

quickly consoled by the promise of more money and a secure future. It is obvious that she is trying to spend as little money as possible on the wedding. She was also trying to keep it secret, but her plan to do the wedding on the cheap by hiring a monk instead of a priest backfires when the monk gets drunk and tells all the neighbours about it. They arrive as wedding guests. Some of them are pious, some are curious, but all present another unwelcome surprise for the mother. Politeness dictates that she welcome them and offer them the cakes that were intended for her son's impending funeral, imposing an unexpected expense.

In this scene Brecht has created a wonderful snapshot (and a bit of a parody) of traditional village life: the mother who arranges everything, the unsentimental bartering about the wedding and its costs, the gossiping neighbours, the need to be hospitable weighed against the expense, and the drunken monk. All these are also the staples of folk comedy that Brecht uses here to show the hypocrisy of 'religious' people, as he did with the character of Aniko, whom we saw earlier. Poor Grusha, whose only concern is Simon's return (p. 50), is all but forgotten. When the time comes to say the wedding vows (p. 51), she tellingly looks at Michael as she promises to be a good wife, since he is the reason for all of this. The peasant appears too sick to answer, so his mother hurries the monk along.

The wedding scene is morbid but also quite funny – the convenience of a dying husband, the financial negotiations and now the monk offering to perform extreme unction (the final rites of the Catholic Church, administered just before death) on the bridegroom right after marrying him, in the hope of making more money. The mother-in-law tries in vain to extract more from Lavrenti, who pays the agreed-upon 600 piastres and leaves Grusha with a final unconvincing show of bravado about his wife and Grusha's next visit.

Brecht uses the conversation between the neighbours – a mix of everyday chat and gossip – to reveal new information to us. We have to follow carefully here in order not to miss clues in the plot: it appears that the peasant woman's son, Jussup, fell ill just when the war started and the neighbours' sons were drafted as soldiers – a suspicious coincidence. Additionally, the mother-in-law mentions that he lay 'like a corpse' after some soldiers rode by, leading her to think his death was imminent and to schedule the wedding immediately. She reluctantly serves the guests the cakes she made, Grusha always willing to help and also trying to keep Michael out of the way.

The mother-in-law objects to the monk's behaviour, and is even more annoyed when she finds out that, in addition to the wedding guests, he has invited his musician friends. His suggestion of a selection of music that would cover both a wedding and a funeral reaffirms the double note of black humour – funny and macabre – evident throughout the scene. Mixed in with the mother-in-law's complaints about the monk, we also hear the possibility that the war is over. Pay close attention here: the stage directions (p. 53) tell us that at this point the dying man sits up briefly. On the next page, the guests confirm that the war is over and the Grand Duke is apparently back in power, with the Shah of Persia lending him military help against the Princes to 'restore order'.

When Grusha hears that the soldiers are coming back, she drops the cakes and staggers with surprise. She is not a demonstrative person, but we can imagine what is going through her mind. She hears that Simon may be returning and her response is to pray, no doubt in a combination of relief, gratitude and anticipation. We see genuine piety in her, in contrast to Aniko with her hypocritical and self-serving attitude, to Grusha's new mother-in-law and even to the monk. But almost immediately Grusha's joy at the thought of being reunited with Simon is

Scene-by-Scene Analysis and Commentary 37

shattered. Hearing that there is no danger of the draft any more, the 'dying' man returns to life, confirming suspicions that he staged his illness to avoid having to fight. Here Brecht tops his criticism of religious piety with a parody of the resurrection of Jesus, complete with a similar-sounding name. Jussup's very first remarks show him to be coarse, unpleasant and just as money-conscious as his mother. His revival also makes for a dramatic and humorous scene on stage, with the mother in shock and the guests scattering before this unexpected figure in his nightshirt who proceeds to eat one of his own funeral cakes. And it is intended to trigger contradictory responses in us – enjoying the comic aspects while realizing that Grusha's future has just become much more complicated through no fault of her own.

An awkward marriage

Time has passed. While Grusha is waiting for Simon, she now has a husband with whom she likely has to share a bed.

Pages 57–8

We see Jussup, the husband, naked in his bath. Grusha is 'playing' with Michael, teaching him to mend straw mats: this is a small but telling detail about not only their poverty but also Grusha's way of bringing Michael up to be helpful and learn useful skills. Jussup acts like a tyrant, ordering his mother about and commanding a reluctant Grusha to scrub his back. He insists on physical closeness while she is trying to avoid it, and complains about her coldness. We sympathize with Grusha, who is caught in a marriage without love, but Brecht makes us see that Jussup, while not a likeable character, does have a point: he is married, he expects a wife to do her wifely duty, including providing sex, and he does not have enough money for prostitutes. So when he says, 'Where you lie, nothing lies, and yet no other women can lie there', we understand that he is also caught in an unfair situation, and Grusha understands it as well, saying that she did not mean to cheat him out of the sexual satisfaction he has a right to expect from a marriage. Then again, he would not have ended up married to her in the first place had he not feigned illness to avoid the draft. Again, Brecht presents a morally ambiguous situation.

The Singer tells us that time passes and Michael grows up. Whenever Grusha washes linen in the stream she remembers Simon, but the memories grow fainter with time, while her marriage – marked by 'evasions and sighs', longing ('tears') and hard work ('sweat', all p. 58) – does not grow easier. We understand that she is refusing to consummate the marriage, remaining true to Simon.

A happy reunion ends in misunderstanding and a dramatic conflict looms

Pages 58–62 Michael is allowed to play with the older children and they re-enact the Fat Prince's coup against the Governor, showing two things: the rebellion we witnessed in Scene 1 has become part of folklore, which typically retells major events in different artistic forms (legends, ballads – and also theatre), and even children do not remain unaffected by what happens politically. In a wonderful bit of irony, the children assign to Michael – the Governor's son – the role of his father. But Michael does not want to be Governor and have his head cut off, and finally they let him do the beheading with a wooden sword. A 'fat boy' acts the role of victim. Later we will see this as an anticipation of things to come. So this little scene of play-acting connects us temporally both to what has gone before and what will follow.

As Michael runs off, Grusha suddenly sees Simon. He is on the other side of the river – a separation that becomes significant as they continue speaking. Grusha's first emotion is joy at seeing him alive and they engage in an exchange that once again is formal but also affectionate and cheerful. Simon, as usual, indulges his fondness for proverbs and the two remember previous scenes of Grusha washing linen by the river. As Grusha hears about Simon's good fortune – he is now a paymaster and earns good pay – she remembers that she struck down an Ironshirt. Simon, knowing her, gives her credit and trusts her reasons, but of course things go beyond that. Grusha is in an impossible situation: she has not forgotten Simon and has remained true to him, but she cannot claim that all is as it was, since after all she has a husband and a child. Simon's understanding has its limits and Grusha despairs about being able to explain to him what has happened, especially across the distance of the stream. Disappointment ensues. As Simon falls silent, the Singer steps in to verbalize his thoughts: he remembers the atrocities and hardships of war, but is unable to communicate what it felt like to fight as a soldier, the way many returning soldiers find it impossible to tell their families what they went through, keeping their feelings inside instead. But we understand how hard it must be for him to come back, expecting to find his beloved and instead realizing that she has broken her promise, married someone else and already has a child by him.

Grusha, understanding how things appear, only wishes he could understand why she had to act the way she did. Her attempts to reassure him about the child – 'But please don't worry, it is not mine' (p. 61) – sound unbelievable to him and he rejects her. Grusha yearns to tell Simon what has happened and to explain to him the hardships she took upon herself to help Michael, which extend to the very situation they now find themselves in. Like Simon, she falls silent, unable to communicate her feelings, and the Singer conveys them to us. If Simon loves her, he should realize that she would help someone in need. While it was difficult – 'I had to break myself for that which was not mine' (p. 61) – she could not have acted differently given the person she is. 'Someone must help!' sums up in an appropriately simple and direct three-word phrase her attitude, and she explains it by images of other living beings that need nurturing to live and grow.

As Simon gets ready to leave, Grusha hopes to keep him by affirming that Michael is not her child. But just then she sees that Michael is being led away by soldiers. In front of Simon, whom she wants to keep from leaving her, she still cannot bring herself to desert Michael. Her answer 'yes' when asked if Michael is her child is simultaneously like saying 'no' to a life with Simon, who walks away.

The Ironshirts leave with Michael, Grusha following him, and the Singer tells us that in the city she will face the birth mother in a court presided over by Azdak.

Important elements of this scene

Two years pass in the course of this scene, which is made possible through the bridging songs of the Singer, who embodies Brecht's Epic Theatre. We see that Grusha's challenges continue. She bears up well under the trials of an unwelcoming family, the humiliation of being forced into a loveless marriage and finally the heart-wrenching meeting with Simon upon his return. We continue to see her strong sense of responsibility for Michael, her determination, courage and occasional stubbornness.

Scene 3 has a lot of comedy, but we can observe that even when Brecht wants us to laugh, his play always has a socially critical edge and offers astute observations about human behaviour. Here some of his criticism is directed towards religion, which he does not portray in a positive light. Piety amounts to hypocrisy in Aniko's case; and at the wedding ceremony religion is presented as something superficial and formal that can be bought as in the 'fifty piastre monk' who only has fifty piastres' worth of piety (p. 53).

The wedding agreement and ceremony are meaningful on

several levels. They advance the plot of the play by introducing a 'solution' for Grusha's situation that will instead turn into a complication. They offer an opportunity for broad comedy, and they also show the hardship of life in poverty in a rural village and the anxieties of an old woman who is worried about money, a hastily acquired daughter-in-law and her own future. Last but not least, we must read the scene as a commentary on conventional morality. Grusha has generously adopted a child left behind and in need of a mother, and she is engaged to Simon, a decent and reliable man who returns her love. But she is despised as an unmarried mother, and in order to be accepted by her family, she has to enter into a loveless sham of a marriage that is only for appearances' sake, based on a financial agreement. As Grusha acts – unhappily – to satisfy the accepted norms of what is right, we are being asked to question those norms.

Her short-lived reunion with Simon is heartbreaking: circumstances whose timing is skilfully engineered by Brecht for maximum dramatic effect force her to choose between personal happiness in love and her responsibility for Michael. There is no solution, but for Grusha there is only one right answer and she makes the sacrifice.

Scene 4: The Story of the Judge

We meet the village scribe, Azdak

The opening of Scene 4 takes us back to the day the revolution broke out. It starts right after the Governor's assassination and the overthrowing of the Grand Duke and runs parallel in time to Scenes 1 to 3. It introduces new characters – especially Azdak, who will play a major role – and at first it appears to be completely independent of what we have seen so far.

Pages 63–6

Azdak, the village scribe, has sheltered an old man whom he saw running away from the village policeman and takes for a beggar. He feeds him, but as he watches his manners and looks at his hands, he realizes with dismay that the guest whom he has sheltered from the police is not a beggar at all but must be of high standing.

We see that Azdak has a way with words and likes to talk. He enjoys speaking in similes and folksy sayings – just like Simon, but is not limited to this register of language. His speech contrasts with that of the old man on the run, who speaks in distinctive clipped phrases – as if his rank and education prevent him from speaking like regular people. (Brecht's model for this style was the way of speaking considered typical of high-ranking conservative German landowners and officers, many of whom supported the German fascists before and during the Second World War.)

Azdak displays mock scorn when his visitor offers him a 'proposition' – an outrageous amount of money for a night's shelter – but then turns around quickly and raises the price. Of course he does not believe the visitor's assurance that the money will be delivered and is about to throw him out when the village policeman, Shauwa, shows up. He reproaches Azdak for having poached a rabbit, which confirms our impression that Azdak is not exactly law-abiding and rejects authority of any kind. Shauwa is no match for Azdak's verbal dexterity and the scribe practically runs rings around the policeman, defending his position on poaching rather outrageously and trying out all kinds of arguments, including Christian theology. His ongoing feud with the policeman is another staple of popular comedy and Azdak is reluctant to hand over his visitor. Instead, he teaches him to eat like a poor man – not simply with greed from hunger but with the additional elements of not feeling safe and having spent too much time without enough food.

Scene-by-Scene Analysis and Commentary   43

Azdak's lesson of how a poor man would care for a piece of cheese following a period of deprivation is beautifully executed, if perhaps not wholly convincing – after all, hunger is a good teacher and anyone on the run would no doubt be eating with rapt attention to food. But Brecht is trying to make a point here, reinforcing the insight that it is not natural to be poor, just as it is not natural to be rich and well bred. (The point is so important to him that, in a later version of the play, he inserted a complementary scene to this one: Grusha, on the run, is trying to act like a noblewoman when she joins three such women on the road. But she is found out because – in contrast to the rich ladies, who are completely helpless – she knows how to clean a room and make a bed, and does it without thinking when it is necessary. Even though she could be very useful to them, they promptly throw her out because she is not of their class, and a fellow servant tells Grusha that nothing is more difficult than imitating a rich and lazy person.)

Many of Azdak's remarks have to be analysed carefully, since his social critique is often rendered tongue-in-cheek or with a peculiar twist. Take, for instance, his remark about the Turkish landowner hanged in Tiflis (p. 66): we might think that his crime was that of mistreating and exploiting his peasants. But Azdak is saying the opposite: someone who was 'merely' abusing peasants would, if anything, be commended for his zeal. The system would never punish a landowner who was mercilessly taking advantage of those under his power. This one was hanged for the 'fault' of being a Turk, not for being an exploiter. Azdak objects when Shauwa attributes good-heartedness to him. Most people would be pleased to be called that, but Azdak complains, 'I do not have a good heart! How often must I tell you I'm a man of intellect?' (p. 65) Here Brecht manages a swipe at intellectuals: it seems intellect and a good heart are mutually exclusive. Azdak's verbal dexterity has its roots in popular comedy; it also seems appropriate and in character for a village scribe, who is by definition more literate than his fellow villagers, if not quite an 'intellectual'.

Azdak takes himself to court

Pages 66–70

When Azdak finds out that his guest is the Grand Duke himself, responsible for countless deaths in battle and among the poor, he is appalled and turns himself in. Note that his relationship with the policeman is such that he can 'order' the policeman to arrest him. Shauwa here starts playing the classic role of sidekick to the main character, Azdak. Azdak denounces himself, offering high rhetoric and exaggerated self-recriminations, and clamours for a trial. He is certain that they are on the verge of a 'new age' of social justice. Even when the Ironshirts point out that they just hanged the judge, he takes it as confirmation of a new social order, where those in power are removed and the power is instead transferred to the people, as happened many years ago in Persia, when peasants, soldiers, dyers and weavers took over. He sings a revolutionary song that expresses outrage at the excesses and ambitions of the rulers, the rich and the military, but frames this outrage within a vision of a new and more just order in which the sons 'don't bleed any more' and the 'daughters don't weep' (pp. 69, 68).

At this point, the Ironshirts enlighten him. It turns out that the rebellion by the Fat Prince, Kazbeki, and the other Princes – which is a political coup of one section of the elite against another – has spurred a popular uprising as well, in which the 'carpet weavers' (representing the working class and therefore the people) were protesting against the lavish lifestyle of the Princes. But the Ironshirts are not on the side of the people. So Azdak had misread the situation and voiced his support for a group in opposition to the Ironshirts. This is an awkward situation for him and he backtracks as quickly as he

Scene-by-Scene Analysis and Commentary 45

can, renouncing his earlier statements and even reversing his self-accusations about the Grand Duke, emphasizing, 'Didn't I tell you I let him run?' (p. 70). Shauwa, now in his role not as policeman but as sidekick and loyal co-villager, defends him. For a moment the situation seems more serious than it turns out to be: once the Ironshirts have had their fun intimidating and humiliating Azdak, the scene dissolves in laughter, Azdak is quite relieved and all of them start drinking together.

Selecting the new judge

The Fat Prince appears, suave and well spoken, his nephew in tow. With an insincere show of respect, he addresses the Ironshirts, summarizes the political situation in a way that is skewed to his own interests and position, and asks them to select a 'very gifted fellow' as the new judge. Conveniently, he introduces his nephew, the 'little fox', as a 'very gifted fellow'. Here Brecht shows us a literal case of nepotism (favouring one's relatives, especially nephews) as the way the ruling class manages to keep power to themselves. It is obvious that the Fat Prince expects the Ironshirts to go along with his suggestion, but feels he has to flatter them and pay lip service to their influence while the Grand Duke is still at large.

Pages 70–74

The Ironshirts see through him and decide to continue their 'fun' for a bit, including Azdak in the discussion. Azdak proposes to test the new judge, but is opposed to doing so with an actual criminal (the Ironshirts have imprisoned the Governor's two doctors). He delivers a speech that displays his characteristic stance: a strong sense of social justice combined with a critique of authority and its automatic acceptance. He argues tongue-in-cheek that the external trappings of the law must be respected precisely because so much of it is arbitrary or directed against people who are acting from need rather than criminal inclination – Azdak gives the example of a woman who has stolen food to feed her child. His statement that 'it would be easier for a judge's robe and a judge's hat to pass judgment than for a man with no robe and no hat' (p. 72) is a condemnation of a system that pays attention to the empty forms of authority rather than actual justice. He offers himself up as mock defendant for the 'rehearsal' to test the Fat Prince's nephew, and assumes the role of the Grand Duke against whom the Princes rebelled, displaying not only his manner of walking but also his clipped speech.

Azdak quickly takes the initiative in the mock trial, rejects the accusation that he started – and then lost – the war and in imperious fashion pretends that he has brought with him hundreds of lawyers. The trial proceeds, with Azdak clearly in the driver's seat throughout. His first move is to declare that he only started the war on the advice of the very Princes who now accuse him. The nephew amends the accusation into 'running a war badly', which Azdak counters by stating that he did not run the war but delegated it to the Princes. He then delivers another of his tongue-in-cheek statements, with exaggerated examples showing that the title of 'commander-in-chief' does not always mean having actual control over things. When the nephew tries to recover the initiative that should be his as (mock) judge, Azdak counters with a detailed and well-informed list of all the ways in which the Princes sabotaged the war. Their main interest, he claims, was to make money out of it, and he has outrageous details and precise numbers at his fingertips to support his assertion.

Brecht's purpose here is to make a historically valid point about war. Regardless of who wins or loses, those supplying the materials will always come out with a profit, while not running any risk for themselves. In contrast, soldiers perish and the population suffers. Thus Azdak's conclusion: the Princes won, in monetary terms, even though the war was lost, and the only true losers were the people of Grusinia, whose rulers were not acting in the country's best interest. At the same time, Azdak challenges the nephew on the language he uses, which is suspiciously similar to the Grand Duke's. Stating, 'Cannot be watchdog if howl like wolf', Azdak reveals the intended nepotism for what it is, and furthermore makes the connection that even though the Princes rebelled against the Grand Duke, ultimately they do 'speak [the] same language' and are equally likely to oppress the people of Grusinia.

The Fat Prince now tries to put an end to the mock trial, still expecting the Ironshirts to go along with his wishes. But instead – having enjoyed Azdak's performance, but perhaps having also been impressed by his arguments – they appoint Azdak. A sense of historical upheaval is expressed in a pun that points to the shortcomings of the judicial system to date: 'The judge was always a rascal! Now the rascal shall be a judge!' (p. 74).

Azdak conducts court cases

The Singer informs us that Azdak served as judge for two years during a period of unrest and upheaval, and we then witness three of the cases that he heard. Shauwa serves as Public Prosecutor – which in the first scene means sweeping the floor and collecting fines. The first case (pp. 75–7) presents two trials that have to be conducted together, allegedly due to the large number of cases due for trial. This process allows Brecht – and Azdak – to establish parallels between blackmail and the practice of medicine, and creates another typical scene featuring the broad – and sometimes black – humour of the popular theatre tradition.

Pages 75–82

We see that Azdak openly solicits bribes, and much of the medical case is about money as well: the case is brought by a rich creditor of the doctor, who had a stroke when he found out that instead of paying him back promptly, the doctor was treating patients for free. As it turns out, it was never the doctor's intention to work for free – he had made a mistake in assuming the patient had already paid. Moreover, he operated on the wrong leg, but Azdak lets this pass as if it were irrelevant. He comments instead on the financial dimension of the medical profession and illustrates with examples how good doctors are at extracting money from their patients. Azdak goes so far as to claim that a merchant sent his son to medical school so that he could learn financial management there.

The extraction of money provides a parallel to the blackmail case: the blackmailer cleverly manages to phrase what is without doubt blackmail in such terms that it appears to be a completely voluntary payment by his victim. Azdak's verdicts are a mix of the ridiculous and the opportunistic, and they too focus on money. He fines the invalid; he advises the blackmailer to study medicine – implying that the medicine that makes doctors rich is simply a different form of blackmail; and he practises blackmail on the blackmailer in turn, taking half of his profits, which Shauwa, in his new function as Public Prosecutor, collects. The doctor is acquitted, since the 'unpardonable error' he committed is apparently an everyday occurrence in Azdak's cynical view of medicine.

The next case (pp. 77–9) is brought by an innkeeper who argues, as he keeps insisting to comic effect, 'on my son's behalf'. He accuses a stable-hand of raping his daughter-in-law, Ludovica, in the stable. As Azdak questions him, we note a subtext: Azdak, who has already taken a bribe from the innkeeper, pointedly refers to one of the horses in the stable, a 'little roan', as 'lovely'; the innkeeper coldly refuses to respond to what is in effect Azdak's interest in an additional bribe. Azdak looks at the beautiful and voluptuous Ludovica closely before questioning her. We cannot help but notice that Ludovica's account of the 'rape' is delivered in highly artificial language and sounds like a script that she has obediently rehearsed and learned by heart. The stable-hand admits he 'started it' – but then, what else could he say without losing his job? Azdak questions Ludovica further and finds that she likes 'sweet things' and physical pleasure. When he asks her to walk across the court and pick up a knife, we can be sure (in fact, we know this from a later version of the play) that she walks swinging her hips and her attractive bottom. And it is her bottom that Azdak in his ruling calls 'a dangerous weapon'. In his verdict, he accuses her of being the guilty party, claims the horse as part of the sentence and promptly leaves the court with Ludovica to 'inspect the scene of the crime' (p. 79), no doubt intending to enjoy her himself.

In this court case Azdak is acting with blatant self-interest, and he is a chauvinist both in painting Ludovica as the guilty party and in soliciting sex from her: today what he does to Ludovica would likely be categorized as 'sexual harassment'. But then again, such scenes are part of a whole bawdy folk tradition of theatre that can, for example, also be found throughout Shakespeare's plays. Moreover, based on the evidence, Azdak is probably correct in deducing that both the stable-hand's and Ludovica's testimonies were coerced by the innkeeper, who wanted to impose his view of what happened rather than admit that Ludovica might have been a consenting party in the adultery. And labelling an attractive bottom 'intentional assault with a dangerous weapon' (p. 79) is certainly an entertaining blend of the physical and legal.

The final court case in Scene 4 is preceded by another performance by the Singer and Chorus. The first stanza explains that during this time of unrest, when there is strife among the powerful ('When the sharks the sharks devour', p. 79), the simple working people have an easier life, escaping scrutiny and oppression. Azdak is described as 'the poor man's magistrate' who carries 'fixed-up scales of justice' instead of practising the proverbial impartiality. But we are told that he uses those fixed-up scales to give 'to the forsaken/All that from the rich he'd taken', like a Caucasian Robin Hood, and that he smiled at 'grandmother Grusinia'. This stanza already prefigures the next court case, as does the third stanza, which states that while brotherly love is to be desired, a show of strength might be more effective and that 'miracles are wrought with axes'.

This is a very public scene, set in a tavern. We are supposed to realize that Azdak travels and sets up court in improvised fashion in the villages: this is justice that is immersed in the everyday life of the people. Three rich farmers are bringing a case against an old peasant woman. Shauwa, as Public Prosecutor, sums up the case, which on the face of it seems crystal clear. There is direct evidence against the old woman: she has been found with stolen property – a cow and a ham – in her possession. There is also circumstantial evidence: when one of the rich farmers demanded a rent payment from her, his cows were killed. The three farmers are like different representations of the same type and they speak practically in unison.

But the old woman presents things differently, like a fairy tale or religious legend: as miraculous compensation for the loss of her son in the war, she has received a cow from 'Saint Banditus'. The farmers respond that of course there is no miracle-working St Banditus. Instead, her brother-in-law, the robber-bandit Irakli, has stolen the cow for her. At this point, the bandit himself, whose reputation precedes him, enters the courtroom, carrying the axe already mentioned in the song. While the farmers are intimidated, Azdak treats Irakli as an honoured guest and goes blithely along with his claim to be a harmless wandering hermit.

The peasant woman continues the narrative that constitutes her defence with another ingenious verbal twist. She cleverly leaves out the crucial role of the bandit in protecting her from the farmers' servants and making the servants turn back as 'bumps as big as a fist sprouted on their heads'. It is the implausibility of her oppressors actually having become good-hearted people that makes her tale so effective. Azdak evidently lends a favourable ear to her distorted version of events, shutting up the farmers when they interject, and the bandit enjoys himself immensely at this version of his efforts on behalf of the poor old woman. She offers, in mock seriousness, her lameness as 'proof' that a miraculous ham was indeed thrown in her window. But her very next sentence returns us to the current of social criticism that runs so strongly through the play, highlighting injustice and economic inequality: 'Your Honour, was there ever a time when a poor old woman could get a ham *without* a miracle?' (p. 81).

In response, Azdak's language turns poetic. He sees in her the embodiment of Grusinia, bereaved and beaten, yet hopeful, and the foundation on which they all depend. One could say that he turns the old woman into an allegory of the country, into a personified image of an abstraction. In a final twist, he sentences the three farmers for 'godlessness', sends them away and invites the 'pious' bandit and the old woman to have wine with him.

This is not justice in the usual fashion – after all, the three farmers were deprived of their property, which ended up in the old woman's possession. Justice is turned on its head when they are additionally fined for not believing in 'miracles'. So, is the whole scene a blatant miscarriage of justice? Most certainly under one definition of justice. But it is justice of a kind within the larger picture, the kind of justice – as mentioned above – that Robin Hood used to dispense, a small instance of redistribution of wealth and goods in a society where this distribution is so unfair to begin with.

This is what the Singer and Chorus comment on in the

following song (p. 82), which addresses the contradictions we see in Azdak and in the court cases presented in Scene 4. Yes, Azdak broke the rules, but he did so to help people. The song blends metaphors ingeniously in the second line: the (metaphorical) 'breaking' of the law is combined with the breaking of bread that provides essential nourishment: 'Broken law like bread he gave them', so that the breaking of the law turns into something positive and life-sustaining. And the song similarly acknowledges that while Azdak does take bribes, he can also 'be bribed by empty hands' – a seemingly paradoxical phrase that captures his way of ruling in favour of those who have nothing, neither for themselves nor to buy his services. Azdak fought the 'beasts of prey', representing those who exploit others, and in order to do so he 'became a wolf to fight the pack': he was an individual fighting – like a wolf, fiercely and perhaps unfairly if necessary – against the larger number and the strong influence of those with power and wealth.

These two stanzas are a celebration of all that Azdak did, in the form of political poetry. They are followed by a much more sober-sounding transition by the Singer alone: after two years, the 'disorder' that allowed Azdak to practise his unique form of law is ending, with yet more violence and bloodshed, and it looks as if things will return to their pre-revolutionary state.

Order returns and Azdak is afraid

Pages 83–5 The stage directions (p. 83) offer us a repetition-and-variation: like the Governor's in Scene 1, now it is the Fat Prince's head that is carried across the stage. Azdak is no longer sitting on his judge's chair but on the ground, engaged in a very everyday task, that of shaving. He has not lost his way with words and laments that Shauwa will no longer benefit from a way of reasoning that may have allowed Shauwa to see the world differently for a while. Now, Azdak fears, Shauwa will return to his foul natural inclinations and, subjecting others to oppression and punishment, 'plant your fat heel on the faces of men'. (Note again Azdak's low opinion of the police, whom he sees not as keepers of order and peace but as instruments of discipline and social injustice.)

He asks Shauwa to sing a 'Song of Chaos' with him in fond remembrance of the times of disorder that allowed for some liberating interference with the old social order. Those 'Who lived always in darkness' were now able to 'come into the light' (pp. 83–4). Of course, the Chorus calling for help from a General is meant ironically from Azdak's point of view, but it describes what has actually happened. Note especially the beginning of the second stanza: remarkably, it refers to Grusha and Michael's fate – which we saw in Scenes 2 and 3. Azdak cannot really know about this, but Brecht includes it for us anyway. With this, he establishes a link from the end of Scene 3 to the approaching Scene 5, where Grusha, Michael and the Governor's wife make their re-entry into the plot. He also encourages us to view what has happened (and perhaps what will happen: these lines can be taken to anticipate the outcome of the final scene) with Grusha and Michael within the larger perspective of social change:

> A nobleman's son can't be recognized now!
> A lady's child can become her slave-girl's son! (p. 84)

But Azdak realizes that the song is about what 'might have been, had order been neglected much longer' (p. 84). (Clearly, Azdak – and by extension Brecht – does not have a very positive view of order, equating its sense of 'tidy arrangement' also with 'social hierarchy' and lack of individual freedom.) The Grand Duke is back, and as usual it is the people who are suffering – their houses are being burned down.

Azdak asks Shauwa to bring him the book containing all the

laws. Even in his dire situation, he is still making jokes, telling Shauwa that he always used the Statute Book (he did indeed: most productions have him sitting on it!). He expects to be punished for having helped the poor and disadvantaged and acted against the interests of the rich, and there is no place for him to hide. He is afraid, and not afraid to show it. This is his mood as the Governor's wife enters, followed – as she would have been two years previously – by the Adjutant. The Adjutant conveys her wishes and Azdak grovels, promising complete obedience. We may disapprove of this, or even hate seeing him so submissive, but Azdak is very human in his contradictions – and besides, his behaviour here influences our expectations for the next scene, when he will be called upon to deliver a verdict in the case. This is the only scene that does not end with a song, which may make us doubly worried about the outcome.

Important elements of this scene

Jumps in time are generally a feature of narratives rather than a dramatic technique. Going back in time two years to a parallel plot is not something plays usually do, so this scene is a good illustration of the liberties Brecht's 'epic' style allowed him to take.

In this scene, the plot of the play really seems to fracture – why on earth are we going back two years, to an entirely different cast of characters? There are two reasons for this. First, Brecht had a lot of fun developing Azdak as a character, and we are likely to share that enjoyment as we learn about him. But we also need to get to know this quirky and original character so that Scene 5 can have the strongest impact on us, and in that sense Scene 4 will turn out to be relevant and indispensable to the plot, even though it initially appears to be an extended digression.

Scene-by-Scene Analysis and Commentary

The three (or rather, four) court cases are entertaining and outrageous, but each of them also highlights specific abuses of power, injustice, oppression and distortion of the truth.

Azdak is one of the most memorable and entertaining characters in theatre. Rogue, Robin Hood, juggler of words and court cases, he cannot but appeal to us as a character, and we are likely to share his sympathies with the underdog and his tendency to argue against those in positions of authority. But Brecht takes care not to make him likeable without qualification: some of his judgements are arbitrary and unfair (the patient in the first case), he acts from self-interest at times (think of Ludovica), he ignores and distorts evidence, and he combines a principled stand (mainly in his support of the 'little people') with a complete lack of backbone in other situations. When it serves his interest, he may be quick to backtrack from the convictions he has only just proclaimed. The court cases do not advance the plot directly and they are largely independent episodes, but they provide a foundation for Azdak's role in the final scene. Not least, Azdak's lack of heroism in the concluding part of Scene 4 sets up our suspense about how the conflict between Natella Abashwili and Grusha will be decided.

Scene 5: The Chalk Circle

Getting ready for court

The Singer opens the scene with a brief summary in the style of an announcement. We see things are serious – Ironshirts are keeping Grusha and Michael apart, and outside the Nuka courthouse the counter-revolution is continuing. Grusha is accompanied by the former cook and Simon. The cook dismisses Azdak as 'not a real judge'. The cook's question to

Pages 86–90

Grusha – why would she want to keep the boy? – acts as a mirror to the advice given to Grusha to leave him behind in Scene 2 (p. 27) and it will be followed by a similar question from the Judge; but now Grusha's response is not just a humanitarian impulse but based on a feeling of belonging. It also gets us thinking about what it means to be a parent. Grusha's reply is simple, and expressed in simple phrases, like an elementary truth: 'He's mine. I brought him up' (p. 87).

We are probably glad to see that Grusha has brought a small 'support team', counting on her side the former Governor's cook and Simon. Both have promised her that they will swear a false oath to help her – because she is 'a decent girl', as the cook puts it. Such lying is of course illegal – we continue here in the line of Azdak's behaviour, breaking the law for the benefit of the poor and disadvantaged. Things between Grusha and Simon are civil but cool. Simon still does not fully understand the situation and is hurt by what has happened, and Grusha mainly has Michael on her mind. Grusha suffers a bad fright when she sees the Ironshirt Corporal whom she wounded so badly when she rescued Michael from him – we recognize him by his dramatic scar. But he pretends not to know her, because admitting that he was pursuing the child on orders of the Fat Prince – who has meanwhile been executed, as we know – would reflect badly on him under current circumstances.

The Governor's wife, Natella Abashwili, enters. Where in Scene 2 she and the child were accompanied by a pair of doctors in her service, now she is accompanied by two lawyers, who are similarly deferential and could be clones of the doctors (in fact the two pairs of characters are often played by the same actors); also by and on her side is the faithful Adjutant. Natella speaks of the 'common people' as if they were vermin. When

Scene-by-Scene Analysis and Commentary 57

the first lawyer warns her to be careful, she answers with obvious insincerity and disdain. Both sides are anxious to find out who will be judge. Grusha and her party need Azdak to be the judge, while the Governor's wife and her twinned lawyers count on him to be replaced. For different reasons, both sides have a low opinion of Azdak.

Once again, we see Azdak in chains. This time, trying to flee, he has been denounced by the three rich farmers whom we saw in court in the previous scene. The Ironshirts subject him to physical violence and are getting ready to string him up and lynch him. The Governor's wife is looking on and applauding with sadistic pleasure.

Here we see yet another side of Azdak: he is probably at the lowest point of his life so far, covered in blood, but he still taunts the Ironshirts, contemptuously calling them 'dogs' (p. 89). At this dramatic point the Grand Duke's messenger arrives with the surprising news that Azdak is the Grand Duke's choice as judge. The Corporal's shout of 'Atten-shun!' is an ironic touch – he does not expect that the message will prevent him from hanging Azdak and, on the contrary, force him to accept Azdak's authority. The reason for the Grand Duke's decision makes sense to us, since we know that Azdak saved his life (although the other characters do not know this); the message is phrased rather mysteriously, but also in a way that shows the Grand Duke's vanity and self-importance.

What we have here is one of those implausible but well-designed coincidences on which theatrical plots often depend. Within seconds, Azdak goes from being the plaything of the Ironshirts, who behave like wolves, to being addressed by them as 'Your Honour'. Azdak himself has never felt permanently elevated by his status; his way of executing the function of judge always had an element of play-acting. Now he remains keenly aware that only by a fluke is he given the robe and

58 Study Guide: The Caucasian Chalk Circle

status. Thus he in turn addresses the Ironshirts as 'fellow dogs' (p. 90). In a few characteristic acts and brief sentences, all of which are orders or statements of intent, Azdak recovers his composure and sees to the completion of his reinstatement as judge: he pardons Shauwa, requests some wine, sends away the Ironshirts, gulps down the wine, asks for the Statute Book to sit on once again – and announces that he will accept bribes. Natella's lawyers greet the news that Azdak will take money as a good sign. Whether their optimism is justified remains to be seen.

The case proceeds: Azdak takes statements from both parties

Pages 90–97 All participants watch Azdak closely – in reading, pay attention to the repeated comments that reflect this, especially from the lawyers and Grusha's ally, the cook, throughout the scene. The Abashwili party willingly pay him more when he hints at Grusha's attractiveness. As if by response, Azdak speaks severely to Grusha for most of the following exchanges. The first lawyer launches into a formal speech and high-flying rhetoric, but Azdak – bringing things down to earth – asks about his fee. Is he speaking ironically when he links the fee to the quality of the lawyers, or does he simply want to see how much is at stake for the rich party in this lawsuit? Either way, the lawyer continues offering flowery language about motherhood as a bond defined by blood. What he says about love and nature in no way corresponds to Natella's actual behaviour. In fact, in her case it was not even necessary to 'tear a child from its mother' (p. 91), as the lawyer puts it, since she herself left him behind.

When Azdak turns to Grusha, her language is in striking contrast to the accomplished rhetoric of the lawyers. 'He's mine' sums up how she feels about him. Her replies are plain and brief; she makes no lofty claims, but states that she did the best she could under difficult circumstances, and that beyond providing him with the essentials (food and shelter, to the extent it was possible for her), she raised him to be a good member of society – 'friendly with everyone' (p. 91) and willing to work. Her use of language also indicates to us that it is hard for Grusha, who is an honest and straightforward person, to lie or even hide part of the truth. She is trying very hard to lie as little as she can and to stick to things she can truthfully say in making her claim – very different from the shameless lies offered by the other side.

Of course the lawyers gleefully point out that Grusha 'doesn't claim any tie of blood' (p. 91); no doubt Azdak would have noticed that anyway. The lawyers and Natella continue in their well-rehearsed presentation that completely misrepresents her feelings towards her child and contrasts sharply with her abandonment of Michael two years ago. We may have begun to wonder why she wants the child back so desperately and the next speech, by the second lawyer, provides enlightenment while also revealing his own true feelings. Natella needs the child for reasons of money and status: he is her only way to retrieve her former fortune and estate. In fact, the lawyer's outrage is mainly self-interest, since they will not get paid unless the estates are returned to her. The first lawyer feels embarrassed about this self-serving disclosure and tries to contain the damage, but Azdak appears not to hold their money concerns against the lawyers. His answer cleverly exploits the double sense of the word 'human', which can mean both 'with warm humanity' and 'humanly weak and fallible'. The lawyer is reassured and continues in smoothly flowing sentences, using the euphemism 'by an unfortunate chain of circumstances' to justify why Michael was left behind.

Azdak now turns to Grusha and questions her with direct

interest in the details of what happened and how. Knowing him, we have some reason to assume that his sympathies may lie on Grusha's side, but his behaviour suggests otherwise, and any inclination to favour her is not obvious to Grusha herself or, for that matter, Natella Abashwili and her party. The answers given by Grusha and her allies – once again – are in direct contrast to the lawyers' speeches: brief statements using everyday language, highlighting different facets of what happened (or what they are claiming happened) that do not fit all that well together. Since Grusha is married to Jussup, but Simon claims the child is his, she also has to swallow the insult of Azdak accusing her of having conceived the child immorally. Azdak's questions about the child – was he from a good family, with 'refined features' – recall today's argument of 'nature vs nurture'. What makes a child the person he or she is? What influence comes from the parents and what comes from the social surroundings? Grusha answers with some impatience, and Azdak displays impatience with her party in turn, accusing them – correctly – of lying and cheating. We may assume that he is taking pains not to appear to side with them from the outset. Grusha panics at the thought of having Michael taken from her, and she and Azdak get into a dispute about his bribes. While she accuses him of being corrupt in the judgements he makes, he berates her for not being willing to pay for justice, as one would for other essentials in life.

Now Simon chimes in and in typical fashion he does so with an idiom. Azdak replies with enthusiasm, and they compete with one another, each trying to outdo the other in clever sayings, several of which offer a twist on the topic of social power differentials. Azdak's displays of verbal cunning are not without vanity. When Simon comes up with a pithy saying to which Azdak cannot muster a riposte, Azdak fines him instead. The tenseness of the scene is increased by the fact that something that unites Azdak and Simon – their common origin in the lower classes and love for folk language – ends up dividing them. Grusha now loses her restraint and passionately accuses Azdak of abusing the law and his position, which Azdak does not deny at all. As she continues, Azdak 'starts beaming' (p. 95) – he has provoked her into a critique of social injustice that is actually very close to his own view and his verdicts as judge. But Grusha does not know this and fears for the outcome of the case.

Azdak then abruptly changes course and interrupts the proceedings to take another case, while – like spectators at a sports match – the two sides assess their chances. The Governor's wife's lawyers feel triumphant; the cook is worried that Grusha (rather than flirting with him, as Azdak suggested earlier) has irrevocably antagonized Azdak by her outburst.

The case Azdak inserts – an old married couple requesting a divorce because they never liked each other – employs an old joke as its punchline. We have seen that Brecht is not above using easy humour in this play; but the case is also introduced for a specific reason, as we will find out shortly.

Azdak now changes his tone again and speaks to Grusha seriously and sincerely, asking her why she would not give up the child, even if he were hers, so that he could benefit from being rich. Here Azdak's words are an echo of the opening lines of Scene 1, which describe all – good and bad – that the Governor had at his disposal.

Once again, the Singer steps in and verbalizes Grusha's silent thoughts and feelings. He explains her conviction that if Michael lived in luxury, he would become cruel and hardhearted, and would show neither respect nor compassion to her and other simple and poor people. We saw that the Governor had to keep many petitioners at bay – here the Singer makes an important distinction when he says, in Grusha's name, that she would rather have Michael fight hunger (his own or that of others) than have hungry men and women as his enemies, the way the Governor did.

Throughout this scene, it is important to note that Grusha never speaks of love for the boy – although we can safely assume that she does love him. But here, for instance, she gives her reason for not wanting to give him up as 'I've raised him, and he knows me' (p. 97). The Governor's wife then notices that Michael is not dressed in fine clothes; Grusha is furious at her insults, and the Governor's wife, by calling her a 'vulgar creature' and trying to attack her, shows us that her apparent refinement is all show and surface.

A test and the final decision

Pages 97–9

Azdak announces that the testimony has not led to clarity about who is the mother, so he will have to put the matter to the test. He places the child in a circle drawn with chalk, asks both women to take one arm of the child, and to pull with all their strength. One of the lawyers objects, fearing that this will disadvantage Natella, who is less used to physical exertion than Grusha – but, as it turns out, Natella 'wins' the contest, to the satisfaction of her lawyers. In contrast to her, Grusha cannot bring herself to inflict pain on the little boy. The test, we realize, is designed to confirm maternal instincts in contradiction to the competitive set-up. It is letting go, not pulling hard, that establishes who acts like a mother, and Azdak surprises both the despairing Grusha and the confident Governor's wife in awarding the child to 'the true mother', Grusha. In a second decision, the judge rededicates the lands that used to belong to the Governor as communal property to the use of all children, to be called 'Azdak's Garden' (p. 98).

Having pronounced the verdict, Azdak is eager to take off

his judge's gown, which has become 'too hot' for him. We can imagine he is speaking not just about the temperature but also about the political 'heat' of having decided against the wishes of the powerful once again. By inviting everyone to dance in the meadow, he is changing his role from official to unofficial. But he carries out one final official act as judge, in which, once again, by getting it wrong and appearing to be muddled and distracted, he is actually getting it right: rather than divorce the old couple, he has divorced Grusha and Jussup, enabling Grusha to marry Simon. We can assume that he has listened and watched closely, formed an accurate picture of the situation and decided to take this additional step to help Grusha and Simon – once again, without overtly proclaiming his sympathies for them. Given his previous conduct and sometimes wilful decisions, it is ironic to hear him state now, with mock seriousness, that judicial decisions cannot be taken back or 'how could we keep order in the land?' (p. 98).

What he imposed as arbitrary fines on Grusha and Simon earlier now appears as a very reasonable fee for his services and Simon pays gladly. And Grusha is finally able to explain that, for her, taking Michael was an act of love that seemed like a logical consequence of her love for Simon and her engagement to him. While everyone is celebrating the happy ending, Azdak vanishes and the Singer sums up one last time, telling us that his time as judge is remembered as 'Almost an age of justice' – not quite perfect, but the best that could happen in complicated circumstances.

Finally, the Singer addresses us directly once more. He links the outcome of the trial to a more general statement and refers back to the Prologue. Here is the parallel to the opening dispute, and the area in which the wisdom of a future society meets the wisdom of the past in what 'men of old' concluded.

The Singer – and by extension Brecht – wants to encourage us to agree 'That what there is shall go to those who are good for it', no matter whether it is children, material things such as cars or land. In this communist and utopian view of an ideal society, one that is based on social and communal responsibility, there are no 'natural' rights to anything, no privileges of ownership or inheritance. Everyone has to prove what she or he is good for; people are judged by their behaviour, not by their status; and they make something their own and establish their right to it by treating it well.

Important elements of this scene

The scene starts out with a dramatic reversal of fortune for Azdak. This makes for good theatre (and reading). It is also typical of revolutionary times and emphasizes the extent to which his having become and being reappointed judge is a matter of coincidence. A shaken Azdak returns to playing a role that has very real consequences: this is almost like a play within a play in that, throughout the proceedings, everything he says and does is closely observed and commented on by the two rival parties.

This is a superbly constructed scene. We know Azdak's political views are likely to sway him towards Grusha's side, but as the case proceeds Brecht carefully builds our expectations and suspense, making it appear more and more likely that Azdak might favour Natella Abashwili. Almost everything seems to place Grusha at a disadvantage: she has no money for bribes, no lawyers, no status and no biological bond to the child, whom she acquired under very unsettled circumstances. The friends supporting her are plainly willing to lie for her. Moreover, as Azdak himself points out, it would be smart of her to flatter him. Instead, she gives brief replies and then starts criticizing him. Then, in addition, Simon beats Azdak in their spontaneous folk-idiom competition. Azdak becomes increasingly impatient with Grusha – everything seems lost. All of this leads up to the moment when the true meaning of the Chalk Circle test is revealed. Up to this point, Azdak has not given away any of his thinking, leaving things in a state of uncertainty that makes us follow with close attention. The outcome is staged quite effectively as a surprise, since it is unexpected for the participants as well, and the effect is heightened by the brisk decisiveness with which Azdak delivers his verdict. It drives home the point – obvious in hindsight – that motherhood means making sacrifices and never deliberately hurting your child. Adding in the divorce makes Grusha and Simon's happiness complete: things end as they should for people for whom we have come to care. The conclusion offered by the Singer brings us back to the larger picture and the moral that the Prologue and the Chalk Circle verdict have in common.

Brecht gives his play a largely happy ending, emphasizing its fairy-tale aspects in the very swiftness of the final reversal. Azdak's decision makes perfect sense to us – so much so that we may not fully recognize the major change Brecht has made to the sources: in his play, it is not the biological mother but the adopted one who proves to be the 'real', 'true' mother.

Brecht's 'Epic Theatre': An Overview

Brecht's plays are important not only as works of art in their own right but also as representations of a particular model of theatre associated with their author. 'Brechtian theatre' and 'Epic Theatre' have become much-used terms in the study of theatre, and Brecht's views on theatre have subsequently continued to exert a great deal of influence on other playwrights and directors.

In the late 1920s Brecht began to develop a comprehensive new concept of theatre. Over the following years, a number of influences came together to shape what he called 'Epic Theatre' or 'anti-illusionist theatre'. This chapter will help you to understand what it is he wanted to achieve. For this, we will start with a brief look at theatre in general and at European theatre before Brecht.

The point of departure: classical European theatre

Theatre is different from prose in one fundamental aspect: stories, novels and other literary prose works all have a narrator – a person or at least a voice who tells us the story – whereas theatre is based on flesh-and-blood actors embodying characters. We do not just hear about what they do; instead, we watch them speak, act and move. The text is intended to be performed and it is either dialogue – words spoken by characters – or stage direction, providing information for the director and actors (and for us, if we read the play). Thus, in the European tradition since the Enlightenment of the eighteenth century, the narrative mode and the dramatic mode are seen as mutually exclusive: the first tells a story, while the second shows it to us.

Brecht blurred these boundaries in his Epic Theatre, going back to the tradition of the epic – long narrative poems performed by a singer-narrator. Its classical form dates back to ancient Greece and it remains alive in many (mostly non-Western) popular folk traditions.

Growing up in Europe in the early twentieth century, Brecht was familiar with the dominant type of European theatre as it had developed since the eighteenth century. This theatre strives to create the illusion that we are watching something 'real' on stage; it is often defined as 'psychological realism'. Interestingly, 'realist' theatre can at the same time be called 'illusionist' theatre, since it aims to provide the illusion of reality.

A number of elements support this illusion on two different levels: the way plays are written and the way they are staged. For example:

- Characters must be complex and psychologically plausible, inviting spectators to believe in them as if they were real human beings, and to identify with them.
- The action should ideally take place within a clearly defined time and a clearly defined place, without interruptions, gaps in time or abrupt shifts. Authorities often talk about the classical unities of time and place. There is a third equally desirable unity: action or plot.

- The action should be coherent and unified, featuring a single set of characters and a continuous plot that is tightly constructed so that events appear to unfold logically, almost inevitably. Plays – whether tragedies or comedies – are usually written in either three or five acts. They follow an arc that leads from an exposition through a complication to a resolution (happy in comedies, unhappy in tragedies).
- The stage itself is enclosed by three walls and is physically set apart from the spectators, who sit on the fourth side. The effect is that of an invisible 'fourth wall' between performers and audience that keeps them apart and must not be broken. In classical European theatre this 'fourth wall' separates us from the events on stage: that is, characters may not address spectators or step outside the magic space of the stage, and the spectators are supposed to be invisible witnesses to what happens on stage, secretly watching and listening, but never commenting or interfering. Only after the curtain falls and the house lights come on is the audience allowed to reassert its presence by applauding the actors.
- Stage design, props and costumes are all realistic, selected with the intention of recreating life on stage.
- Lights are dimmed during performances, heightening the illusion and making the audience largely invisible to the actors.
- Actors aspire to embody the characters they represent to the point of 'becoming' the characters and disappearing completely inside them. (This acting style came to be known in the USA as

'method acting'; it still dominates the Hollywood film industry, which is in many ways comparable to non-Brechtian European theatre in the way it seeks to establish an illusion of realism and provide spectators with opportunities for identification and empathy.)

Epic Theatre as a way of developing a new audience

For a number of reasons, Brecht became critical of this form of theatre. He felt it reduced spectators to the role of passive consumers who uncritically accepted their entertainment. Brecht believed in art that followed a classical double ideal of combining 'education and entertainment' and he felt that the most important step towards achieving this would be to disrupt the illusion that allowed spectators to sit back and relax rather than think about what they were seeing on stage. Further, he hoped that theatre could have an influence on how people saw society and encourage them to build a society that would offer more justice for everyone. He wanted to engage their intellect on two levels: getting them to think first about his plays and then about society, both the way it was and the way it could be. Brecht's ideas on theatre are thus a combination of aesthetic and political thought – thinking about art, but also about society. His theatre is always political. For him, art had to have a social message and push people towards thinking about how to improve the social and political situation. In one of his poems – written in exile, after he fled from fascist Germany – he talks about how easy it would be to just enjoy the beautiful and harmonious things in life and put them into poetry. He describes how in his mind the pleasure of seeing a tree in bloom competes with dismay about Hitler's latest speeches, but says that only the latter urges him to his desk.

The concept of Epic Theatre differs from classical European theatre in a number of ways. Brecht did not want to further an illusion or give the impression that what was shown on stage should be taken as real. He did not want spectators to identify with the characters uncritically – rather, he wanted a balance of identification and critical distance that would be conducive to thinking about the play. He wanted theatre to be not just an emotional experience but also an intellectual one that would provide insights and opportunities for critical thinking. Going beyond that – and here his views of theatre were influenced by such political and philosophical thinkers as Karl Marx and Georg Wilhelm Friedrich Hegel – he did not want spectators to accept characters' actions as inevitably determined by human nature. Instead of highlighting the universality of being human and assuming that humans were basically unchangeable, he saw theatre as a kind of laboratory for investigating human behaviour in detail.

Brecht's political thinking was strongly rooted in the philosophical tradition of dialectics, which – put very simply – emphasizes contradiction and the ways in which contradictory elements can often be shown actually to belong together. He became interested in the contradictions that marked human character, individual behaviour, social phenomena and political developments. He was not interested in presenting a plausible chain of events that by virtue of unfolding smoothly would appear inevitable. Consequently, his focus was not on presenting characters as coherent, universal and constant. He was convinced that humans could change, and be changed, depending on the world they lived in, and that their very ways of thinking were shaped by, and specific to, their social position. For Brecht, history played an important role, and he always wanted to emphasize that humans acted in accordance with circumstances, that they were not independent from historical conditions and that there were alternatives to their behaviour and actions. He wanted to use theatre as a way of making his audience think about behaviour – and society – as both conditioned and changeable, to change them from passive consumers into engaged and critical spectators.

Anti-illusionist theatre

All of this led Brecht to develop a model of theatre that was based not on illusion and emotional identification but on distancing the audience and on breaking the illusion. In order to encourage spectators not simply to accept what they saw unthinkingly, Brecht realized that he had to disrupt the double process of illusion and identification that was so dominant in theatre at the time, and he came up with a number of ways of doing this. Much of his thinking drew on traditions that either came before the establishment of the 'classical-realist' model or were found in non-European cultures. Shakespeare, for instance, combines realist elements with clearly non-realist ones: his plays can span decades, there are multiple plots, characters not infrequently address spectators – breaking the 'fourth wall' in the process – and we know that the Shakespearian stage used fairly minimal scenic design and props, relying instead on words to let spectators know what they were supposed to imagine. Similarly, there are numerous theatre forms – both in folk traditions, often orally transmitted, and in highly artistic kinds of acting and playwriting – in Asia, Africa and in European countries that are not based on illusion and have no 'fourth wall' to break, since there is no formal separation between performers and audience in the first place. Brecht himself was strongly influenced, for instance, by seeing Chinese actors in the 1930s perform in a highly stylized way that did not rely on the actors' identification with the characters

Brecht's 'Epic Theatre': An Overview 73

they represented but instead 'demonstrated' behaviour and actions. Brecht liked this style because it turned action from something natural into something 'strange'. From this experience he developed the idea of *Verfremdung* and, with it, the so-called *V-Effekt*. Literally, this German term means the effect of 'making strange' or defamiliarizing (although it has at times been misleadingly rendered in English as 'alienation' or 'alienation effect'). Making something unfamiliar and thus strange, the *V-Effekt* is produced by taking something out of the realm of the habitual, the unquestioned, and making it remarkable, surprising, worthy of questioning. Defamiliarization is both a mode of presentation and a mode of responding to something: it interrupts our automatic acceptance and makes us think. In this way, it combines distance with surprise.

Brecht was often faulted for wanting to do away completely with identification and empathy. But the author knew – or quickly realized – that emotional investment was a human trait that could not easily be eliminated. As he explained in numerous texts, what he wanted was a combination of both. He objected to the uncritical way spectators would watch mainstream theatre: 'Yes, I've always felt that too' – 'This is natural' – 'Everything is plausible here, so this is great art.' As he summed up this uncritical response, they would agree with what they saw, laughing with the characters and weeping when they did, accepting their misfortunes as inevitable. What Brecht wanted was the opposite; for spectators to feel (or rather, to think and feel): 'I would not have thought that' – 'This is strange, almost unbelievable' – 'This has to stop.' He wanted them to feel that theatre was great art precisely because nothing that was shown could be taken for granted, and to be moved by a character's plight not because there was no solution but because it would actually be possible for him or her to find a way out. He wanted the ideal spectators of his Epic Theatre to be able to laugh at a character who was weeping, and to weep at laughing characters – and then to think about why they were laughing or weeping.

The *V-Effekt*: Techniques of distancing and defamiliarization

Brecht's Epic Theatre employs a number of identifiable techniques to achieve the effects of distancing (preventing uncritical emotional identification) and defamiliarization (making something appear strange, puzzling, worthy of thought). Some of them (see A, below) apply to the construction of his plays and some of them (see B, below) to their staging. All of them serve the dual purpose of distancing members of the audience and making them combine critical thinking with an emotional response.

A

In the way Brecht writes his plays, we find numerous distancing techniques. For example:

- Many have an episodic structure, in which individual scenes may have a considerable degree of independence, rather than the tight causality and inevitability that move a traditional European play so convincingly to its resolution and conclusion.
- Some of his plays are open-ended, or he wrote different versions with different endings, making any individual ending less inevitable.
- Many of his characters break the invisible 'fourth wall' of the stage and address spectators directly.

Sometimes this is done in a prologue or epilogue, but it can happen throughout the play.
- Brecht liked to combine showing and telling. In several of his plays, he used the technique of introducing a scene with a brief summary. Its purpose combines orientation for the audience with a lessening of our tension/anticipation, so that rather than figuring out what actually happens, we can pay more attention to how it happens and why – and, just as importantly, how it is presented. Brecht's hope was that providing these 'previews' would liberate his audience from becoming too caught up in the scene.
- Another way of including narration in his plays that was frequently used is the addition of a narrator or commentator to the cast of characters. By talking to the audience, such figures break the 'fourth wall' and bridge the divide between the actors and the audience. They make it more difficult for members of the audience to identify with characters on stage as if they were real. A narrator can take on a variety of tasks, such as providing background information, explaining, externalizing a character's thought processes, asking questions, commenting or summarizing (either after events have taken place or in anticipation). A narrator figure can provide both orientation and transition as the action on stage switches to a different set of characters or location. This device is frequently employed by Brecht to move beyond the restrictions that the traditional Western 'three unities' (of time, place and action/plot) impose on what can be presented on stage.

- Frequently, Brecht's plays include a chorus. Taken from ancient Greek theatre, the collective voice of the chorus combines the functions of comment, warning, clarification and anticipation of events to come.
- Finally, defamiliarization also works in the way characters' thoughts or opinions are presented. You will find numerous examples in *The Caucasian Chalk Circle*, and several are discussed in the following chapter, '*The Caucasian Chalk Circle* as Brechtian Theatre'.

B

At the level of staging his plays, Brecht (and followers of Brechtian theatre) had a number of favourite techniques to achieve the *V-Effekt*. For example:

- He frequently used posters and banners bearing statements in order to disrupt the illusion of the stage as a separate and self-contained world.
- Rather than the traditional curtain that effectively marks the place of the 'fourth wall', he preferred a low and semi-transparent curtain that allowed the audience to see the scenery changes.
- In Brechtian performances, either the lighting might be non-realistic or lights might not be dimmed in order to keep the audience from assuming the customary position of sitting unobserved.
- Actors might change into or out of character in full view of the audience, or one actor might play several characters quite openly, as another way of deliberately alerting the audience to the way the

actors were presenting characters rather than embodying them.

Finally, one significant and characteristic feature of Brecht's form of theatre is found at the intersection of writing and staging, of text and performance: many of his plays include songs and music, which serve to interrupt or comment on the action. Their effect of breaking the illusion of realism is not unlike that in a musical, though with a much stronger intention to provoke political enlightenment, and with much more aesthetic variety. The songs in *The Caucasian Chalk Circle* will be discussed in detail in the following chapter.

Gestus and showing internal processes

It comes with Brecht's general distrust of traditional realism that while he likes to focus on individual character traits, he is for the most part not strongly interested in giving us psychologically believable, well-rounded characters. He is more interested in characters' actions than in their essence. For him, a character is part of an experimental constellation, and his intention is to present (and ask) how someone would react under specific circumstances. Moreover, he was not interested in making his actors 'disappear' behind the façade of the character, but instead wanted them to 'present' the characters while remaining visible as actors. He liked to point out that the 'reality' of a play was precisely that of having actors move around the stage showing characters to us, and he wanted the audience to remain aware of this act of showing instead of getting caught up in the presentation. He would remind his actors, 'You have to show the act of showing.'

One of the challenges in theatre is that a character's inner processes, unless they can be shown clearly by body, gestures and facial expression, must be verbalized, while in prose narratives a narrator can helpfully explain to us what goes on within a character's mind. For Brecht, theatre was very much about externalizing inner processes, showing a character's stance or attitude in everything that character did. He called this the *Gestus*, which for him could be shown in facial expression (unless of course actors were using masks), in gestures, in the way characters moved or positioned themselves. Importantly, it is also expressed in the language his characters use. Showing a *Gestus*, then, does not require the actor to slip into the skin of the character; it is closer to demonstrating a particular attitude or response. The *Gestus* always had a social dimension for Brecht: it was not simply psychology, but helped illuminate the force field of power distribution and relationships. Thinking of *Gestus* as Brecht used it helps us to understand that Brecht considered speaking a form of action. His characters do not just utter words: they argue, flatter, criticize, correct, accuse, insult, defend themselves or others, explain, apologize, try to persuade someone, refuse to do something, and so on. This is why it is very important to pay attention to the rich variety of language in Brecht's plays and to how different characters use language.

Old or new?

Brecht wanted a radically new theatre, one that broke with everything that had happened in so-called classical Western theatre since the mid-eighteenth century, that shook its foundations and established an entirely different model, based not on illusion and identification but on observation and defamiliarization. He aspired to a theatre that shifted from emotions and psychology to demonstration and argument, that featured episodic plots and that, in presenting social reality, elicited 'intervening thinking' and political action. Another view is that Brecht drew upon a long tradition of anti-illusionist theatre, in the West and beyond, in order to highlight a political awareness and social criticism that had already been in evidence in theatre. For this view, the attention he devoted to making visible contradictions, complexities and conundrums in innovative ways on stage had always been what theatre was about at its core. The truth, as usual, lies somewhere between the two positions and combines aspects of both, depending on which feature of his theatre one emphasizes in one's argument.

The Caucasian Chalk Circle as Brechtian Theatre

Not only is *The Caucasian Chalk Circle* a splendid play in its own right, but it is also significantly shaped by Brecht's thoughts on theatre and by his model of how theatre should be conceived and the effect it should have on its audience. This chapter will help you to connect the previous introduction to Brecht's 'Epic Theatre' with *The Caucasian Chalk Circle*, providing numerous examples and allowing you to develop a richer understanding of the play.

The actors
The core of the play, Scenes 1 to 5, are performed as part of what we see in the Prologue and are framed by its discussion. Even though we never return to the Prologue, Brecht wanted us to keep that setting in mind throughout. Usually, a number of characters from the Prologue will remain on stage as spectators. Scenes 1 to 5 are thus presented as a 'play within a play', and the audience that would be visible on stage throughout reminds us, as spectators, that we are watching a play, something that is being deliberately shown to us. Brecht himself countered the expectation that theatre should provide an illusion of showing us something as if it were happening in 'real life' by saying that the reality he wanted to show was that of actors who were physically present on stage and modelling

characters for us: again, he wanted to emphasize the 'showing of the showing'.

The text states that the Singer arrives with four musicians for the performance. But we see many different characters on stage – so either the musicians keep taking on different roles or the members of the fruit collective are joining the Singer and his musicians to perform the play for their guests. Brecht liked the second version, which means that the actors playing some of the peasants in the Prologue will now be playing some of the *Chalk Circle* roles – in other words, they will be playing peasants who play the roles of Grusha, Azdak (who in turn plays the role of the Grand Duke in the mock trial), Simon, Ironshirts, and so on. On stage, we would probably see them openly changing into costumes for these roles (this kind of decision is made by the director of any given production and can vary). Many of the *Chalk Circle* characters are poor and simple people, like the peasants. But they will also play the roles of the Governor and his wife, the doctors and the lawyers, the Fat Prince and the Grand Duke. So we have actors playing poor peasants playing rich and privileged characters, and also have a peasant playing Azdak in his tattered clothes giving a performance of the Grand Duke and all his airs. As you can probably see, this is a great way for Brecht to use *Verfremdung*, since the layering of characters will prevent us from taking them as 'real' or 'natural'. Staging the play this way, as Brecht wanted it, combines illusion and the breaking of illusion.

For another level of distancing, Brecht employed a traditional technique of classical Greek and folk theatre: he had the actors – or rather, the peasants – in the play use masks to portray some of the characters, especially the high-class ones. Masks are very useful to show them as stereotypes rather than individuals, and to prevent empathy and identification (not that we would be particularly tempted to identify with the

Governor's wife or the Fat Prince). They are also helpful in showing *Gestus*, the attitude of a character, rather than trying to establish psychological or emotional subtleties, since they force the actors to work not with their face but with their whole body, taking up certain positions, walking in a certain way, relating to others with their body (threatening, pleading, accusing, explaining, and so on).

Plot structure

Brecht rather flagrantly disregards the classical European model of the three unities of time, place and action in this play. The Prologue is supposed to anchor *The Chalk Circle* as a performance, but there is a good chance that we will lose sight of the frame, especially as readers, as we follow the fates of Grusha, Michael, Simon and Azdak. Only the very final words bring us back to the Prologue. Nor is there anything to connect the two main characters, Grusha and Azdak, before the final scene. In Scenes 1 to 3 we hear and see Grusha's story, which unfolds in various places in Grusinia and seems to extend over several years (much more like an epic than a regular play). We find out in the next scene that it must be two years, for at the beginning of Scene 4 we suddenly jump back two years, back to the revolution we witnessed in Scene 1, and are told what at first appears to be a completely unrelated story about the judge, Azdak. Note also that the Singer introduces Scene 4 as 'the story of the judge'. Brecht introduces Azdak at length because we need to appreciate his character and the verdict he will deliver at the end, but also because he is such a splendid and eccentric character that it would be a shame to bring him in only at the end. Scene 5 finally ties together what up to that point have been two parallel but separate stories. Some critics have complained that (counting the

Prologue) the play offers three different and largely separate plots.

Brecht, as stated above, liked episodic plots rather than tightly woven ones. In a certain sense, this play's plot is actually *less* episodic than some of his other plays: what happens to Grusha and Michael has a sound logic and persuasive causal development – one step follows from another. Scene 4, however, is an instance of Brecht's preference for the episodic: it really does not matter in which order Azdak hears his three cases, and we do not know when exactly he does so during his two years as judge. It is good, though, to have the 'Granny Grusinia' case last, because it emphasizes Azdak's tendency to rule against those with more money and power, which is why he is afraid of what will happen to him once the old regime is back in place.

Brecht's preference for episodic over dramatic structure does not prevent him from paying close attention to plot structure. The final scene of the play is prepared carefully through the verdicts Azdak renders previously and the seemingly haphazard way he sometimes reaches his decisions. The divorce case of the two old people in Scene 5 seems silly and irrelevant, merely a way of stringing out the suspense, until we realize that Brecht has introduced it in order to set up the final harmonious resolution.

Characters and language

As stated before, Brecht was not particularly interested in creating well-rounded and fully plausible characters. He felt it more important to diagnose contradictions and scrutinize interactions between characters than to create heroes or heroines. When we look at the characters in *The Caucasian Chalk Circle*, we can easily see that a number of them are not particularly complicated. The Governor is rich, spoilt and arrogant;

someone who takes pleasure in his power and a life of luxury, and is not a good ruler. The Fat Prince is also interested in power, and is better – at least for a while – at obtaining it via political manoeuvring and strategic alliances. The Governor's wife is not a 'rounded' character at all – she is spoilt, hysterical and self-centred.

The two doctors – and the two lawyers – are caricatures, comically simplified figures whose function is to show how character-deforming it is to be uncritically obedient to those in power. Their attitude – the *Gestus* of utter subordination – also shows the power of those whom they serve. Brecht wants us to see that unjustified power corrupts both those who wield it and those subordinated by it.

Simon Shashava is straightforward and reliable, sometimes a little slow to understand, and the seriousness with which he performs his duties, even when they go against his self-interest, may be worthy of praise but may be perhaps a little foolish. So while he is certainly likeable, and we see him as a good match for Grusha, he is not idealized. In fact, while the members of the nobility seem to have no redeeming features, almost all other characters – even the minor ones – defy classification as completely good or bad.

This is true even of Grusha, easily the most positive character. In fact, Brecht found it difficult to make her appear less than good and noble. But he wanted her to come across as somewhat stubborn, acting from a sense of what is right, but also because she has limited powers of imagination. He did not want her to be seen as the embodiment of selfless generosity and 'natural' motherliness. Thus her planning to give Michael up and her complaints to him that he is costing her a lot need to be taken seriously. Brecht also wanted us to see how difficult it is simply to do the right thing under challenging circumstances.

Often minor characters are used to make specific points. For instance, for Brecht the old man who sells Grusha milk at an outrageous price is not simply greedy; he is also poor, put out by the war like everyone else. And Brecht carefully shows the different stages of response and different attitudes of the peasant woman who takes in Michael. We see one *Gestus* when she first notices him, another in the way she talks to her husband, yet another set of *Gestus* as Grusha tries to reason with her to protect the child, before Brecht finally captures her fearfulness towards the Ironshirts (which is justified, but also distinguishes her from Grusha, who has a firmer attachment to the boy and is thus willing to risk more).

Even fairly simple characters are used by Brecht to stage contradictions. Aniko can be seen as a truly one-dimensional character, but also as someone who demonstrates the strong influence of rigid village morality. Many of these minor characters cannot simply be characterized as either good or bad. Lavrenti does not share his wife's moral narrow-mindedness so much; he is simply a coward. Yet, in his own way, he does want to help his sister and thus comes up with the marriage plan to remedy the situation – and that, in turn, leads to a number of plot developments. Jussup's mother is not particularly likeable, but she also shows the influence of utter poverty on one's behaviour.

In Scene 4, Brecht has fun with a number of characters, some of whom have their roots in folk comedy. The Grand Duke – fleeing without a penny, but still expecting to be able to buy favours, and with the characteristic speech of the upper classes – provides an entertaining little scene that is put to excellent use later when Azdak imitates him. While we can certainly criticize Ludovica's trial for its sexism, the character of Ludovica – naïve, voluptuous, intimidated by her father-in-law – is an enjoyable creation, as is the fearsome bandit Irakli, who pretends to be a humble beggar and is moved to tears by the fate of a poor old woman.

And, finally, Azdak is one of the most satisfying characters Brecht has ever created, in the tradition of the smart trickster, rascal or jester figure, who plays a prominent role in many folk tales. Azdak has certain firm character traits: he sides with the underdog, he has an ingrained distrust of authority, he loves to provoke others, he is agile in his thinking and has a clever way with words. He is a chameleon, able to inhabit and play multiple roles.

But he also embodies a number of major contradictions, several of which are pointed out explicitly in the text. We see him taking bold stands and defying people in power. But he also values his own life and at times betrays his principles. He is both courageous and cowardly. Twice we see him retreat quickly from an uncomfortable position: when he misunderstands the Ironshirts' position on the revolution (pp. 69–70) and when he assures Natella Abashwili of his obedience (p. 85). He is not the least interested in appearing courageous or heroic, but only in saving his skin. This is much more realistic and frankly human than many acts of heroism depicted in literary texts, and it is also in line with Brecht's own conviction that heroism was only called for when the social or political situation demanded it. In his *Life of Galileo* we find a brief exchange on the topic. When Galileo's student Andrea says, 'Unhappy is the country that does not have heroes', Galileo objects with a variation on the same sentence that shifts our understanding of the role heroes play: 'No. Unhappy is the country that is in need of heroes.' This is also a perfect example of Brechtian *Verfremdung* (see below for more). Brecht overturns our usual valuation of 'heroism' from something noble and good to something that points to a problem and a lack.

Returning to Azdak's contradictions, he is corrupt and solicits bribes – but he often rules against those who bribe him, letting himself instead be 'bribed by empty hands'. He has a strong sense of justice, even if it goes against the letter of the law. He indulges his self-interest (such as when he demands a horse in the Ludovica case). He is wily and can act strategically, but he also miscalculates at times (such as when he praises the revolution to the Ironshirts). He appears to exploit his position of power (as judge) for his personal enrichment, but at the end his underclothes are still torn (p. 89) and he has clearly not amassed any personal wealth. After the final court case, we see him sitting with Shauwa and shaving. Brecht later changed Azdak's task in this scene to that of mending his shoe, to underscore how little Azdak amassed in bribes during his two years as judge.

As the final scene shows very clearly, while Azdak appears to be distracted and muddle-headed, he is actually very good at seeing and extracting what matters. Even though he pretends that he divorced the wrong couple by mistake, it seems much more likely that he understood what was going on with Grusha and Simon and decided to put things right for them as well. We may remember here Azdak's speech about the correct outer form of the law, which does not prevent it from imposing injustice on people (Scene 4, pp. 71–2). Azdak violates the outer form of the law in numerous – often comical – ways, but he still manages in many cases to arrive at the heart of the matter with his judgements. In characterizing what made Azdak different from other judges, Elisabeth Hauptmann, one of Brecht's collaborators, insightfully summed it up by saying that he was an 'incorrect supplier of justice' rather than a 'correct supplier of injustice'. Even if he is in many ways not a traditional hero – often showing cowardice – he becomes a hero to the people of Grusinia.

The Caucasian Chalk Circle as Brechtian Theatre 89

Given that Brecht claims not to be interested in eliciting psychological subtlety and complexity, the language his characters use is of major significance. In creating what we can think of as their linguistic profiles, he draws on a remarkable range of language registers. As a writer, Brecht shows a diverse set of influences in his use of language. They include Martin Luther's pioneering translation of the Bible into German in the early sixteenth century (Brecht cited the Bible as a book that had had a major influence on him), southern German dialect comedy, nineteenth-century melodramatic ballads, and literary and non-fiction works from many languages and cultures. Brecht also had an excellent ear for how people spoke in everyday situations or on the street.

In *The Caucasian Chalk Circle*, we find the imperially commanding language of those in power and the language of workers and peasants, we find folk wisdom and false piety, we find language used to intimidate, to mislead and to hide true motives, among other things, and we find frequent shifts from the everyday to the poetic through song. Azdak has a considerable repertoire of language styles at his disposal – from sermonizing to a degree of profanity that mirrors that of the Ironshirts. He can speak formally and informally, bending language to hide his position or to display it with passion. His use of language is highly variable.

Language was closely connected to a character's *Gestus* for Brecht. The play presents a wide range of stylistic forms, used in creating characters, in establishing instances of defamiliarization, in giving the play a poetic dimension and in unmasking characters. See how the subservient language of the doctors ceases once their employers are no longer in power (p. 21), and how insincerely the Fat Prince expresses his alleged willingness to defer to the Ironshirts' decision, with political motives skewing his account of the revolution (pp. 70–71). Note how Azdak deliberately mimics the Grand Duke's clipped speech (p. 72–4), and how the Fat Prince's nephew inadvertently falls into the speech pattern of his class (p. 74). Remember how Ludovica gives herself away in her testimony by speaking as if from a script with artificially formal language (p. 78); and how the language of the lawyers and Natella keeps changing during the course of the trial in Scene 5, in which they play a public role but intermittently betray their actual feelings and goals. The striking contrast between Natella Abashwili and Grusha in Scene 5 is established by their use of language. Similarly, if not quite as dramatically, earlier in the play we can observe the difference in the way two soldiers, Simon and the Ironshirt corporal, speak.

Realism and *Gestus*

For Brecht, the stage was a laboratory for examining reality. Thus we have complex characters and stereotypes; we have close attention to detail (How do two servile doctors bow to their superiors while simultaneously engaging in competition? How does a poor person draw money from a purse? How does a spoilt landowner's daughter walk?), but also rather flagrant breaks with what is usually considered a convincing and plausible imitation of real life.

The bridge over the abyss which Grusha negotiates with Michael could not be staged realistically – it would be difficult to present an abyss on stage. The exchange with the three merchants before she braves the abyss serves to reinforce the urgency and Grusha's desperate situation – and yet Brecht has Grusha pause and sing a little song of resolve to Michael. Her song, telling him she accepts the danger and suffering that they will have to face together, interrupts the stage illusion. It is highly implausible that Grusha – who had no nappies for

Michael and almost no money – would have managed to walk for twenty-two days on her flight, but Brecht does not bother to give us any details to make this more convincing. While Jussup's motivation for hiding in bed and pretending to be ill is believable, it is certainly not realistic that he would be able to fool everyone – including his own mother – for an entire year. And how realistic is it that Azdak can not only imitate the Grand Duke to perfection but also has war-profit statistics at his fingertips? How would a village scribe have come by this kind of information? It is left to us to decide whether Azdak invents these numbers or has them at his command in a rather flagrant violation of plausibility. Brecht does not mind such inconsistencies and breaks in the degree of realism. On the contrary, he considered them an important element of the distancing at work in Epic Theatre and he designed them intentionally, entirely in keeping with his view of theatre.

Rather than present wholly plausible characters or portray an overall state of mind, Brecht was much more interested in showing a specific *Gestus* in specific scenes or utterances.

Some characters have one or two basic *Gestus*. The two doctors, for instance, combine subservience towards the Governor's wife with hatred towards each other. But *Gestus* can also be employed flexibly and in a way that gives clarity to what the characters do and how they do it. Take, for instance, the moment in Scene 2 where the peasant woman finds Michael and decides to take him in (pp. 34–5). This can carry a different *Gestus* in virtually every sentence: the woman dismisses her husband's unhelpful remark about the priest, expresses the beginning of attachment to the child, asks a question that shows she is uncertain, weighs the options pragmatically, delights in the child's smile, which confirms the attachment, and comes to a decision which she communicates to her husband in a tone that does not allow any protest.

The scene where Azdak acts the part of the Grand Duke is another good example of making the Grand Duke's *Gestus* observable and of employing defamiliarization. The portrayal of the imperial arrogance and way of speech of the Grand Duke by the dishevelled and shabby-looking Azdak creates the maximum contrast between the two characters and shows that the Grand Duke's behaviour is a pretence rather than a fixed personality trait.

Verfremdung/Defamiliarization

'Making strange' in Brecht operates at many different levels. Understood as distancing the audience from identification and uncritical emotional response and breaking the illusion of witnessing immediate reality, it is represented in this play by such devices as the narrative summaries at the beginning of scenes, the Singer's comments (see below) and his characters' way of speaking. Framing the 'Chalk Circle' play by the Prologue is an important level of defamiliarization; having it acted by the peasants – and, moreover, having them play different roles in the course of the performance – also distances us, as does the continued presence of on-stage spectators (the peasants, but also the peasants acting as neighbours in the Jussup scene and as onlookers in the Irakli/'Mother Grusinia' scene), who remind us that what we are seeing is fake. But defamiliarization is also evident in Grusha's untimely song before attempting to cross the abyss with Michael. And the engagement scene between Grusha and Simon, performed slowly and calmly in the midst of a chaotic revolution, makes us stop and think about what an engagement really means.

But *Verfremdung*, as noted above, is not only meant to

distance us by the way scenes are set up; it is at work in how the characters express themselves too. For example:

- When the Singer at the end of Scene 1 speaks of 'the seductive power of goodness' (p. 29) as though it were a vice, we are forced to reassess our usual valuation of goodness – to think about it differently, and also think about a situation that makes it so dangerous to do good.
- Simon's insistence that quarrelling in a crisis is to be avoided since one 'needs time for a good quarrel' (p. 22) is surprising: quarrels are not usually approached rationally, and the idea of a 'good quarrel' (in keeping with the assertion about the pleasure of disputing in the Prologue) is counter-intuitive.
- The imagined call of the baby to Grusha (p. 28) goes very much against our expectations: rather than plead for help, as we would expect, he presents Grusha's helping him as an act of self-preservation for her. We need to stop, take note and think about ways in which this might be true, forcing us to think more deeply about the meaning of the play.
- Grusha's reminder to the peasant woman that the Ironshirt is also someone's son (p. 37) instantly changes her – and our – view of the soldier.
- The language in which the blackmailer presents his extortion of money transforms it into a voluntary and generous exchange (p. 76).
- The manner in which the old peasant woman in the 'Mother Grusinia' court case (pp. 80–81) describes what actually happened as a 'miracle' by leaving out a few crucial details turns a beating by Irakli into a miraculous conversion.

- When Azdak berates Grusha for not bribing him and disapproving of the custom, he defamiliarizes our accepted view of bribery as contemptible (p. 94).

In all these examples, familiar concepts are turned on their head. We are puzzled for a while, and the turn – outrageous, clever, provocative – forces us to consider new aspects of something we thought we knew. This, too, is *Verfremdung*.

As you can see, the effect that results is similar to that of the punchline to a joke. In Brecht, *Verfremdung* and comedy can be closely linked and their effects reinforce one another. Both rely on something suddenly appearing in a new and different light, or being presented from mutually exclusive points of view. You can observe this in Scene 3: often what is welcome from one perspective (a nearly dead husband for Lavrenti and Grusha) may be distressing from another (Jussup's mother). Jussup's 'resurrection', for instance, is quite funny, but also spells heartbreak and difficulties for Grusha. The wedding scene provides particularly good instances of Brecht's intention, summarized above, to make us laugh when characters cry and cry when characters laugh. Brecht wants us to notice these discrepancies and the significance of different perspectives, nudging us to adopt a critical view of what happens instead of merely being entertained or assuming there is only a single way of responding.

The Singer and the songs

In his Epic Theatre, Brecht likes to combine theatre and storytelling. *The Caucasian Chalk Circle* is an excellent representation of this. Scenes performed by the actors are mixed with songs, and frequently include passages of (sung)

The Caucasian Chalk Circle as Brechtian Theatre

commentary by the Singer, who is not playing a character but is one of the major figures of the play. Song is an important characteristic of Epic Theatre, since it often interrupts the action and reminds us that what we see is imaginary. Brecht frequently uses songs to provide brief summaries of the scenes to come. But it is important to note that in *The Caucasian Chalk Circle* he uses songs flexibly and with a great deal of variety. There are about forty, most of them sung by the Singer (sometimes joined by the Chorus), and they are a major element of the play. With the exception of the Prologue and the end of Scene 4, every scene both opens and closes with a song. The following overview of individual songs in the play complements the earlier Scene-by-Scene Analysis and Commentary. It concludes with a summary and will help you both to understand individual songs and to appreciate the many different ways Brecht incorporates them into this play.

Scene 1
Singer: 'In olden times...'

The first song is a textbook example of Brecht's distancing technique and his infusion of theatre with 'epic' storytelling. Here we have the Singer in the classical role of narrator, standing outside the action. Note that the Singer is using a 'well-thumbed notebook' and a style of recitation that shows he has performed this many times before. In other words, rather than create the illusion of immediacy, Brecht wants to highlight that this is a (repeat) performance. He wants us to feel not like witnesses of history in the making but like a generic audience.

Page 13

This song could be the beginning of an epic about the Governor, but it is in fact used to set the stage in our imagination and take us to a specific time, event and scene. It both introduces the churchgoing scene and 'doubles' it – we hear about the petitioners and soldiers, but we also see them. This means that we are not totally dependent on the upcoming scene but are given two modes of interpretation. While the song sounds like an old legend, it expresses a modern political sensibility towards class and social oppression.

Singer: 'The city is still . . .'

Page 16 The song provides a transition from one scene to the next, interrupting the continuity of theatrical illusion and introducing two new characters to us. In this brief song, too, the Singer acts as narrator. Here he provides a neutral preview and summary. In other plays as well, Brecht used the technique of introducing a scene with a brief summary. Its purpose combines orientation for the audience with a lessening of tension or anticipation, so that rather than anticipating *what* will happen, we can pay more attention to *how* it happens.

Singer: 'The city is still . . .'

Page 18 The first line is the same as in the previous song, but the continuation is different. Now the Singer asks questions designed to arouse our curiosity and alarm. The tone here is ominous and dramatic. As he announces that dramatic events are disrupting the stillness, the Singer shifts from 'why' to a relentless 'and . . . and . . . and' in combination with a parallel structure of 'not . . . but' that uses precise images (the goose that is cooked but not eaten); both techniques are found frequently in oral epics and folk narratives.

Singer: 'O blindness of the great!'

Page 20 Here the Singer's language becomes more elevated in tone and more political. His declamation includes the powerful image of great men walking on the bent backs of their subjects. He condemns those holding power for their practice of oppression and their naïve reliance on a perpetual continuation of their

The Caucasian Chalk Circle as Brechtian Theatre 97

status, and he celebrates the coming of change that will improve the fate of simple people.

The action continues while he speaks, and he addresses the Governor directly – another break in stage illusion – using dramatic contrasts such as promising him a coffin and grave instead of a new palace. Then he shifts our attention to the servants for the following scene, combining statement and commentary with the poetic image of 'sweating oxen' (the servants) going down with the wagon as it plunges into the abyss.

Grusha: 'Simon Shashava, I shall wait for you . . .'

This is the first of several songs sung by one of the characters, as part of the action but simultaneously bringing the action to a temporary standstill. Grusha's folk songs run parallel to Simon's use of folk sayings. The two characters are defined linguistically and politically as representatives of an authentic folk tradition and of the lower classes. Rather than promise Simon her true love in plain words, Grusha does so by song, in images and traditional repetitive phrases that combine the beauty of oral tradition with her character's sincerity about the engagement.

Page 23

Singer: 'As she was standing . . .'

One of the challenges in theatre relates to verbalizing the inner processes of characters. Here the Singer takes on that function of narrator and speaks for Grusha as she stands still, conveying her thoughts and reactions as if from inside her mind – 'so it seemed to her' – so that she does not have to verbalize them. In contrast, the Singer can use a subtle and detailed vocabulary to convey her emotions to us. Within the song about Grusha, speaking for her in detailed, descriptive words, the Singer also verbalizes what Grusha ostensibly – and of course impossibly – hears the baby say to her, speaking in his own mature voice and using the language of folk poetry. We must

Pages 28–9

imagine Grusha showing her emotions in her facial expression, revealing her inner state as well as her reponses to what she hears the child say. The Singer sums up an evening and night, accelerating time in a way that is impossible for actual stage action, until he finally tells us the outcome. At the end, his words work in parallel to what we see.

Scene 2

Page 30 **Singer: 'When Grusha Vashnadze left the city . . .'** *and* **Chorus: 'How will this human child escape . . .'**
Grusha: 'The Song of the Four Generals'

Pages 30–31 This scene opens with not just one but three songs. First, the Singer gives us a brief and rather bland summary of what follows in the opening section. It is left to the Chorus to spell out – in a dramatic way – the danger Grusha and Michael find themselves in. As they echo the Singer's words, they expand on them. Interestingly, both the Singer and the Chorus give Grusha's singing equal weight with her action – buying milk – pointing to the general importance Brecht accords music and singing in this play.

While these two songs belong to the 'epic' narrative framing of the theatrical action, the next one is sung by Grusha as part of that action, walking with child, stick and bundle. This presentation of singing is realistic and plausible, not part of Brechtian distancing. Grusha may be singing to keep up her energy and also to entertain Michael, perhaps in order to stop him from crying.

Singer: 'As Grusha Vashnadze . . .' *and* **Chorus: 'How will the barefoot girl escape . . .'**

Page 32 These songs provide a transition to the scene that follows, which introduces us to the Ironshirts pursuing Grusha. As on page 30, the Singer provides the dry, factual commentary, while

The Caucasian Chalk Circle as Brechtian Theatre   99

the Chorus adds tension, emphasizes the danger and provides dramatic colour through language ('Butchers').

Ironshirts: 'Sadly to war I went...'
This is another song that is integrated into the action, sung – appropriately – by soldiers sent to war. On one level it is a simple and sentimental folk song about true love and death in war. It emphasizes once again that nothing good will come of war for the simple folk and lowly soldiers. On the other hand, given the soon-to-be-evident cruelty and sexual exploits of the Ironshirts (or at least the Corporal), the idea that a loved one will be kept safe by one's friends is probably not credible. The charming little song acquires an ironic dimension given the brutal behaviour of the Ironshirts and the task they have been given.

Page 33

Singer: 'When Grusha Vashnadze came to the River...'
The Singer summarizes Grusha's exhaustion and the need to come to a decision about the child, making it clear that time has passed. Here he contrasts poetic language with the realities of Grusha's flight: 'the rosy dawn/Is cold to the sleepless one, only cold'.

Pages 33–4

Singer/Chorus: 'Why so cheerful...'
Here the Chorus speaks for Grusha in reply to the Singer's two questions to her, which emphasize her conflicting emotions: she is both cheerful and sad, feeling both relief and loss at having given up Michael.

Page 35

Singer/Chorus: 'Run, kind girl!'
In a few lines the Singer provides dramatic tension, telling Grusha what to do. In contrast, the Chorus distances us from the acute danger with its generalizing statement about 'kind people' in bloody times.

Page 36

Study Guide: The Caucasian Chalk Circle

Singer/Chorus/Grusha/Singer: 'And in her flight...'

Page 39   The Singer again compresses time – in this case, twenty-two days – and along with the Chorus (which emphasizes that both Grusha and the child are 'helpless') provides a summary of what happens next. The adoption – presented more like a baptism – is then told in the form of another song, sung by Grusha. It is through the songs that we understand what is happening and that we see actions that are symbolic, not practical – Grusha pouring icy water over the child and taking the fine linen off him. The final portion of the song, sung by the Singer, provides a bridge to yet another place and time. As in the opening song of this scene, Grusha's singing a song is mentioned explicitly, given equal importance here with the danger she accepts.

Grusha: 'The Song of the Rotten Bridge'

Page 41–42   This song, sung by Grusha as she gets ready to risk both her own life and Michael's, sounds like a traditional folk song but is tailored specifically to their situation. Thus, rather than having Grusha utter some emotional words, it suspends the dramatic action, making sure we do not succumb to breathless tension, and reminds us that we are watching a constructed scenario. Unlike Grusha's singing as she walks, this song provides the prototypical Brechtian epic-distancing effect of suspending the action and breaking the illusion of realism, even though it is sung by a character. In contrast to the dramatic situation, the last of the three stanzas is relaxed, even humorous in tone.

Grusha: 'The Song of the Child'

Pages 42–3   Here Grusha once again sings to Michael, the way mothers do, as part of the action on stage. Now that she has in effect taken on the role of his mother and is not just a temporary caretaker, it seems particularly appropriate that she sings – addressing

The Caucasian Chalk Circle as Brechtian Theatre 101

him directly – about his origins and his future. Beautiful metaphors help create the tone of ancient folk poems when Grusha calls Michael 'the tiger's son' and 'the son of the snake', emphasizing the contrast between his parents and his own behaviour: he will be gentle and compassionate, not continuing their arrogance and self-centredness but offering help to others.

Scene 3
Singer: 'Seven days the sister . . .'
This song combines functions we have already seen: it compresses time and prepares us for the coming scene by presenting Grusha's unspoken thoughts and expectations. But here the preparation sets us up for a surprise, since Grusha's expectations are not met. It also provides a foil that allows us to judge her brother's less than brotherly behaviour even more clearly, while at the same time giving us a hint as to why he may be acting in a cowardly manner and in deference to his wife, whose wealth he has married into.

Page 44

Singer: 'The sister was so ill . . .' *and* Grusha: 'The Song of the Center'
The Singer summarizes what happened and compresses time – at least half a year – for us. The final three lines shift to a voice that combines those of the characters.

Page 47

We then shift back directly to the action on stage, with Grusha singing to Michael as she works. Her song of survival in war brings together her thoughts of Simon and a lesson to Michael as part of his education.

Singer: 'The bridegroom was on his deathbed . . .'
A pointedly laconic and impersonal summary that encapsulates a scene that is complex, introduces several different characters and is in turn funny and tense.

Pages 49–50

102 Study Guide: The Caucasian Chalk Circle

Singer: 'O confusion!'

Page 56   Here the Singer's summary, again moving through time, is wryly detached as he outlines Grusha's complicated situation, torn between three different obligations and allegiances (to Simon, Michael and Jussup). Grusha wants nothing less than to 'discover' that she has a husband, but is forced to do so through her marriage vow and physical proximity. Pay attention to the song's rhythm: the final two lines have a beat before 'The bedroom is small' which makes the everyday statement both funny and ominous.

Singer: 'As she sat by the stream to wash the linen . . .'

Pages 57–8   A folk-song-like interlude takes us back to the scene of Grusha washing the linen and Simon watching her from Scene 2 at the same time as it compresses time, taking us many months into the future. Unemotionally, the Singer briefly refers to the dissatisfactions of Grusha's marriage to Jussup. The speeding up of time goes hand in hand with a typically Brechtian emotional distancing.

Singer: 'So many words . . .' *and* 'There was yearning . . .'

Pages 60–61   The Singer speaks both *to* us ('Hear what he/she thought . . .', pp. 60, 61) and *for* the characters ('what he/she thought but did not say . . .', pp. 60, 61), expressing what they are unable to express themselves in this crucial scene. He allows us to see the different points of view of both characters and enter into their thoughts, which makes it clear to us why their communication breaks down at this point. The Singer adopts first Simon's and then Grusha's perspective and language, making them clearly parallel by using similar formulaic language and folk-style repetitions. We can imagine Simon's state of mind as he returns from the cruelty and deprivation of war, expecting Grusha to have kept her promise. We understand Grusha's inability to plead with him for understanding and we sympathize with her wish that he could have trusted her to do the right thing and remain true to him even in a situation that seems to suggest the opposite. Brecht did not want these songs to 'interrupt' or 'distance' the action, although the Singer's presentation is sufficiently unusual to have that effect on us. Mainly, though, they were intended as a poetic interpretation of the silence of misunderstanding and were meant to give expression to the thoughts and emotions of two straightforward characters whose strengths do not lie in communication. Here Brecht would have expected the actors to show in their faces the emotions – suspicion, reproach, disappointment – that are expressed in the song.

Grusha's song uses the typical repetition-with-variation of folk songs in 'the battle . . . the bloody battle, the bitter battle', along with the alliteration of the repeated b's. Several sentences begin with 'I had to': this repetition of the same phrase at the beginning for emphasis is a poetic device called anaphora. The closing lines of her song use similes taken from nature and country life that express solicitude.

Singer: 'The Ironshirts took the child . . .'

At the end of Scene 3, the Singer's concluding lines combine sober summary with emotional accents ('the beloved child', 'the unhappy girl', 'the dreaded city'). Again, we find several repetitions of words or structures, typical of the formulaic folk tone. The Singer asks no fewer than five questions, in this case raising our expectations about what will happen – even though Scene 4 first moves us back in time before the action continues in Scene 5.

Scene 4
Singer: 'Hear the story of the judge...'
Page 63 Here the Singer again embodies a traditional narrator as, this time, he moves back in time at least two years, to the beginning of the revolution. The summary orients us in time, tells us accurately what we are going to see next and focuses our attention on a newly introduced major character. While finding out about characters – how they act and why they do so – is of course one of the major pleasures of watching plays in the theatre, the way the Singer puts it here is much more typical of prose narratives and oral epic storytelling. It is another prototypical reminder and indication of the 'epic' character of Brecht's play and his whole approach to theatre.

Singer: 'Thus Azdak gave the old beggar...'
Page 66 The Singer provides a bridge in time, but also his summary bridges the scene we have just seen and the scene to come, and clarifies their causal connection.

Azdak: 'The Song of Injustice in Persia'
Pages 68–9 The song advances the action since it drives home Azdak's revolutionary attitude to the Ironshirts and prompts them to query and then threaten him.

In retrospect – after Azdak has been intimidated and made to recant his revolutionary opinions – it is funny to see him belting out this song, with Shauwa's 'Yes, yes, yes...' as the chorus.

But in celebrating the revolution and prospects for social justice in Persia, it also expresses the possibility of rebellion in poetic language rather than political terms, reinforcing Brecht's conviction that poetry could be a force – and a weapon – in the fight for a better society.

The Caucasian Chalk Circle as Brechtian Theatre 105

Singer: 'And there was civil war . . .' *and* **Singer and Chorus: 'When the towns were set afire . . .'**

The Singer's first lines are a laconic summary and preview in prose of the next two years, followed by a much more colourful verse description of the situation and announcement of Azdak's rule, making us curious about how precisely Azdak is going to conduct himself as judge.

Page 75

Singer/Chorus: 'Men won't do much for a shilling . . .'

This is a continuation of the earlier verse preview (p. 75) that introduced Azdak's first appearance as judge. In the same form – rhymed, rhythmical – and like a second stanza, it introduces his second case, this time highlighting the elements of bribery and corruption, and the fact that Azdak helps those who are too poor to bribe him.

Page 77

Singer/Chorus: 'When the sharks . . .'

The song that began before Azdak's first court case and continued with the second carries on here with three more stanzas. It is funny and metaphorical, characterizing Azdak in general while also anticipating the last of the three court cases. The continuation of this song in instalments that introduce each of the three court scenes also serves to provide continuity and tie together all three cases.

Page 79

Azdak: 'Granny/We could almost call you . . .'

It is a measure of Azdak's rather extraordinary and unconventional performance as judge that here he bursts into poetry while working towards a judicial verdict. It is also another instance of Brecht interrupting the stage illusion with a patently unrealistic poetic interlude that temporarily shifts the court case to a different level. The end of Azdak's recitation comes

Pages 81–2

close to a prayer, before he changes linguistic register abruptly again and condemns the plaintiffs.

Singer/Chorus: 'And he broke the rules...' and Singer: 'But the era of disorder came to an end...'

Page 82 Two more stanzas from the Singer and Chorus complete the song about Azdak and his court cases, bringing this major section of Scene 4 to a conclusion. The song in its entirety is boisterous, energetic, provocative and exuberant, featuring lively language that celebrates Azdak as an agitator against the status quo. The stanzas feature strong and original images and complex sentences, with a dynamic rhythm to the lines and a rhyme scheme of AABCCB for each stanza.

The Singer continues by himself, moving us through time to the end of Azdak's two years as judge. We notice a conspicuous contrast in tone and language, reminding us that the Singer's passages fulfil a variety of functions. The sentences are brief, sometimes very brief, and syntactically very simple. The language is pointedly neutral and factual, offering a set of plain and separate statements without any opinion. All verbal exuberance is gone and the brief account is foreboding in its restraint, as befits the plot.

Azdak (with Shauwa): 'The Song of Chaos in Egypt'

Pages 83–4 This is another song that Azdak sings in character – suspending the action, but not as an interruption by an outside voice like that of the Singer or the Chorus. The song demonstrates with a number of parallel examples the changes in fortune that people have experienced. But unlike the Persian song he sings earlier, this one refers quite specifically to what happened during his time as judge and mentions – rather surprisingly – Michael's fate (see also Scene-by-Scene Analysis and Commentary), thus

The Caucasian Chalk Circle as Brechtian Theatre 107

reminding us of previous events and guiding us towards the final scene.

Scene 5
Singer: 'Hear now the story of the trial...'
The scene opens with the kind of announcement-summary ('Hear now...') in four lines that we have already encountered repeatedly, giving us the gist of what we are about to see.

Page 86

Singer: 'Hear now what the angry girl thought but did not say...'
This song is comparable to the two songs in Scene 3 where the Singer verbalizes Grusha's and Simon's unspoken thoughts and feelings. Its three stanzas have a simple light metre and regular rhyme (AABB), presenting Grusha's position in an almost naïve form – similar to a song one might sing to a child – that contrasts with the importance of what she has to say. Note that Azdak responds to Grusha directly afterwards, as if he could hear her thoughts, such is the effect of the Singer's intervention. In a realist play, this would feel odd – in Brecht's non-realist style, it is perfectly acceptable.

Page 96

Singer: 'And after that evening Azdak vanished...'
The final word belongs to the Singer. Here the Singer functions like an omniscient narrator in a novel who can look into the future. The final lines are directed towards us, exhorting us as listeners (or readers) to 'take note' of what is presented as the moral of the play in a final breaking of stage illusion and the 'fourth wall'.

Page 99

Summary

The most important musical performer is without doubt the Singer, mainly in his function as storyteller (narrator) and commentator. Brecht uses him to break the illusion of 'showing reality' and to do things that in classical European realist theatre would have no place on stage. There are many ways in which the figure of the Singer enriches our experience with the play and helps us to understand the meaning of what happens.

The Singer sings for the audience on stage, but also for us. He does not respect the 'fourth wall'. He can talk to us directly and by doing so interrupts what is happening and reminds us intermittently that we are watching (or reading) a play. As an observer, he also models our own role as spectator and serves as our stand-in or representative within the play. He can address us or the characters, or he can speak for the characters.

He can set the stage for the next scene with his words, comment on the action in a general way or tell us what we see as we see it, and perhaps explain it to us (such as Grusha's adoption of Michael, p. 39). Often he introduces characters to us, so that we do not have to figure out who they are but can instead pay attention to how they behave. Very frequently, he orients us in advance of a scene with a brief preview. He can provide summaries of what we have just seen or what we are about to see, guiding our expectations, and he can offer a general conclusion or interpretation of the specific events we witness (like a reader making sense of a text).

He plays an important role in offering transition and orientation as the action on stage switches to a different place, time or set of characters (remember that Brecht preferred 'individual' and separate scenes to the seamless logical and temporal flow of one scene into the next favoured in classical European theatre). He manages shifts from one scene to the next, and this function enables Brecht to disregard the 'three unities' (time, place and action) of classical European theatre while making sure that we understand the plot. He can compress and accelerate time or help us to jump forward or back and fast-forward through periods of time (hours, months, even years) that it would be impossible to present on stage (no one wants to see twenty-two days of Grusha's wandering in real time!). In this way he is able both to support and to disrupt the temporal continuity of what happens in the play.

On the one hand, the Singer can distance us emotionally from the action – this is a characteristically Brechtian function. But he can also provide dramatic tension (at the end of Scene 3, p. 62, he does both). He can ask questions and make us curious. He can raise expectations in us that may then be either fulfilled or disappointed (as they are at the beginning of Scene 3, when Grusha arrives at her brother's home). He can present memories and provide lessons (for instance, p. 47). Since he is not a character, the Singer has an almost unrestricted number of verbal and musical registers at his disposal. He can switch from prose to poetry and include elements of folk songs. His songs can tell us about the characters in a more distanced way than their own words, but also at times more insightfully. And last but not least, he can articulate for us the unspoken thoughts and emotions of characters, giving us deeper insight than they themselves could (he does so for Grusha and Simon at their reunion in Scene 3, and for Grusha's unspoken reply to Azdak in Scene 5).

This last function does not necessarily distance us. For that reason, it would be simplistic to think of the songs exclusively as a means of *Verfremdung*. The same thing is true for the songs sung by the characters which may have realistic motivations:

to sing while walking, marching in step (for soldiers), cheering oneself up or entertaining a small child. But even these songs must be read carefully, since many contribute to our understanding of the play. They can, for instance, provide an ironic counter-perspective to what is happening: this is the case with the pleasant, simple song the Ironshirts sing (p. 33) as they pursue Grusha and Michael.

Conclusion: Major Themes and Overall Interpretation

We can think of Brecht's *Caucasian Chalk Circle* as a fairy tale about social justice. The play has a timeless dimension. Scene 1 begins with the formula of a fairy tale, 'In olden times', and it shares with fairy tales the happy outcome for the underprivileged. Those who act decently receive their just rewards, the bad characters are punished. Fairy tales are to a considerable degree about social justice – the kind of justice that in life does not prevail nearly as often as one would like – so the comparison of this play with a fairy tale is quite appropriate.

But the play is also anchored in historical and social specifics in a number of ways, beginning with the Prologue that sets up the theme of how traditional wisdom, laws and customs must be subjected to examination and tempered by new insights as times change. Given the extent to which the Prologue is tied to the communist order in the Soviet Union, it has sometimes been criticized as the 'socialist wrapping paper' for what would otherwise be a pleasantly ahistorical play. But we know that Brecht considered the Prologue essential for the larger points he wanted to make, and the closing lines of the play emphatically direct us back to the question the Prologue asks, rather than leaving us with a generic 'and they lived happily ever after'.

In Brecht's work, social injustice along with the abuse of power is a constant preoccupation and his impulse towards his work is strongly political. The 'Chalk Circle' play itself – Scenes 1 to 5 – is quite specific in portraying social inequality. Its society is modelled on a feudal system in which the peasants are exploited, the poor have little opportunity to improve their lot and the rich live in splendour based on that exploitation. The ruling elite is represented by characters who have few, if any, redeeming qualities: the Governor is more interested in further enhancing the level of luxury of his life, leaves his soldiers to deal with the poor and cannot even be bothered to attend to political unrest, which causes his destruction. His wife is spoilt and hopelessly self-centred. The Fat Prince is a schemer interested in power, not in the people. The ruling classes are also shown to be resistant to change (unless it is to seize more power) and unreformable. Natella Abashwili cannot stand to be around ordinary people ('I can't stand their smell. It always gives me migraine', p. 88). And just as the Fat Prince suggests in Scene 1 that a doctor should receive physical punishment or be killed if an illness surfaces (p. 16), in the final court scene Natella shows her incomprehension of an actual justice system by reverting to her pre-revolutionary behaviour, invoking her feudal and arbitrary right to give orders for physical punishment, when she screams in reference to Grusha, 'She's a criminal, she must be whipped. Immediately!' (p. 97) Their lackeys – especially the doctors and the lawyers – grovel at the same time as protecting their own self-interest.

All the likeable characters come from the underclass. Grusha and Simon have only minor flaws – stubbornness and an inability to attend to their own self-interest, which is hard to even consider a flaw. They are practical, dependable, straightforward and loyal. Azdak is a much more complicated case, as we have seen – but without a doubt he is an engaging character with a strong sense of social justice.

Conclusion: Major Themes and Overall Interpretation 113

The minor characters from the lower classes provide an interesting illustration of Brecht's views on social justice. Many of them act in less than appealing ways – they are greedy, selfish, cowardly. But in each case Brecht emphasizes that they act from a position of poverty, and thus makes sure that we at least glimpse at some justification.

Our first case in point is the old man in Scene 2 who extorts two piastres from Grusha for the milk. He is taking advantage of Grusha's need, but he is also a victim of the soldiers. Lavrenti is another case. He has married into money – an understandable way of securing a decent lifestyle. Now he is paying for it by being under his wife's thumb and having to play along with her insincere piety and moral rigidity. At least he comes up with a way of helping his sister. Jussup's ruse of dissembling illness to escape military service is understandable – rather than getting drafted into a war that has no advantages for him and endangering his life, he finds a way of protecting his own interests. (Remember how Grusha argued with Simon in Scene 1, wanting him to act with less heroism and more concern for his own life? She would probably have liked him to have an element of Jussup's sense of self-preservation.) Even his mother, who appears thrifty and calculating, can also be seen as a resourceful poor woman trying to get by with a desperately ill son who cannot contribute to the work needed to make a living as a peasant. Finally, the old woman in Azdak's last court case in Scene 4, who strictly speaking is profiting from stolen goods, is presented in a contrasting light as well. A situation of pervasive social injustice – conditions that keep the poor in dependence and do not allow them to better their circumstances – is addressed in one blessed and redeeming instance.

Brecht was a materialist: he insisted that ideas, thoughts, opinions and convictions were rooted in concrete social conditions, and he was intent on portraying that causality in his plays. He always wanted to show the role played by money quite openly, by having it not only mentioned in the text but also frequently displayed on stage in the character's actions. The play offers numerous examples of this. In Grusha's milk purchase, we must imagine her opening her purse with hesitation. The stage directions read: '*She fishes a long time in her bag*' (p. 32). She takes so long to extract the two piastres from her purse not because she cannot find them, but on the contrary because the purse is probably nearly empty, and Brecht wants us to think about that as we watch her spending what money she has on Michael. On a related note, Brecht wanted the actor portraying the old man to bite the coins, to make sure they were genuine.

We have seen that, for Lavrenti, the differential in wealth in his marriage strongly affects his behaviour: it gives his wife the right to dictate even how he can treat his own sister. And the marriage scheme he comes up with for Grusha is presented in financial terms – he surreptitiously takes his wife's milk money, showing that what is a small amount of money for Aniko is a significant sum for Jussup's near-destitute mother. We see the latter's ploy to get even more money than the negotiated sum of 600 piastres from Lavrenti when, hoping to trick him, she asks, 'Did we say seven hundred?' (p. 52). And the scene also spells out the other conditions of the marriage contract, reminding us that the old woman has to make sure she has a place to live when her son dies and will not be thrown out by a new daughter-in-law she has little reason to trust. Lavrenti assures her, 'You'll have it in writing that the farm will go to you: but she'll have the right to live here for two years' (p. 50).

Each of Azdak's cases either focuses on money directly or addresses social inequality in some other way. His indictment

Conclusion: Major Themes and Overall Interpretation 115

of medicine as being mainly a way of making money, akin to blackmail, resonates with us after we have seen the two doctors in Scene 1 callously abandon the child (and his mother). The old woman in the 'Mother Grusinia' case sums up the social injustice that provides the larger framework for any individual decision about justice in her plaintive remark: 'Your Honor, was there ever a time when a poor old woman could get a ham *without* a miracle?' (p. 81). Brecht was fond of such reversals of customary points of view, which were part of his technique of *Verfremdung*.

Azdak is unashamed about soliciting bribes because he likes to bring the topic of money out into the open, as when, for instance, he asks Natella's lawyers in the final scene how much they are being paid. But he also provides an important perspective on the bribes he takes with his outburst in that scene, when he condemns Grusha and Simon for criticizing him as corrupt. Azdak's reproaches to Grusha (p. 94) may seem counter-intuitive at first. Are we seriously being asked to consider bribes and fines as necessary elements of justice? But Azdak's arguments – and his surprising parallel between justice and the meat one buys at a butcher's – make us see that while 'justice' is an abstract ideal, it has to be administered in social-material reality through a court system, and one must expect to pay for it just as one pays for other essential goods and services in life.

When we think about it this way, collecting bribes and fines (modest or substantial depending on the party's ability to pay) is like setting up a basic finance system for justice. Getting justice without paying would mean that judges could be recruited only from among the powerful and wealthy, who might not be disposed to rule in favour of those without power or money. Azdak points out that ideals have costs (just as we see the tangible and intangible costs of Grusha's devotion to Michael), and he reminds us that justice does not appear from nowhere; it relies on his work and thus he needs to be financed in some way. Here Azdak is not simply saying that justice should not be free. He is pointing out that any court system is bound to cost money, and that this cost should be borne by everyone in society, because that is the best way of preventing the system from being biased towards only those with the money to run it.

This interest in money and its importance precisely for those who have little of it, and who may not be able to afford justice in a system that privileges the rich in everything, is a way of ensuring transparency. It is very different from the greed that motivates Natella Abashwili, and that makes lawyers who are fundamentally indifferent to the actual merits of a case engage in lofty rhetoric on behalf of undeserving clients, eager merely to extract their hefty fee. But we also see that Azdak is not unsympathetic to the necessity of earning one's living. So, just as he insists that the law must have a proper financial basis, he finds the lawyers' desire to get paid perfectly understandable even if they have been hired by an unscrupulous woman. Brecht famously stated his view that ideals usually took a back seat to the material necessities of life when he said, 'First comes food, morality second.'

Another recurring motif in the play is war. Brecht lived through two world wars, he read political analyses of the First World War, and in this play he wanted to convey a clear sense of how war affects those engaged in it.

What we have in *The Caucasian Chalk Circle* is a rebellion of one power elite against another. Briefly summarized: the Governors serve the Grand Duke, who wages an unsuccessful war against Persia; the Princes, who supposedly support the Grand Duke in his war, rebel against him and his Governors;

Conclusion: Major Themes and Overall Interpretation 117

the Grand Duke flees to Persia and the Shah of Persia lends him an army to restore order and do away with the Princes.

Brecht's point: social class, not nationality, decides one's allegiance (this is why, historically, the workers' movement had such a strong international component). Wars are about profit and power, not the interests of those who make up the ordinary population of the countries at war. The Princes show just as little interest in social welfare, wishing to keep the people in a state of servitude. Their rebellion is a power grab, not an attempt to change anything else in society. The Fat Prince, Kazbeki, calls the working classes 'those eternal troublemakers' (p. 70), and Azdak's mock defence in Scene 4 shows that the Princes are not only devoid of any patriotic feeling (such as Azdak and Irakli manifest in the 'Mother Grusinia' case in Scene 4), but have actually sabotaged the war and caused countless lives to be lost because they were acting to maximize their own profit. This particular reading, which has sound historical-political foundations, illustrates the lesson that not every rebellion leads to social change, and wars and revolutions usually mean hardship for the common people. The Singer makes this point at the end of one of his songs (p. 20) and Grusha chides Simon for his misplaced loyalty and for taking soldierly obedience too far in times of rebellion (p. 22). The old man selling Grusha the milk pointedly tells her, 'Kill the soldiers if you want milk' (p. 32). This point turns him and Grusha from antagonists to common victims of the war.

There is more. We see and hear about Ironshirts committing atrocities and being prepared to inflict violence. Taxes on the poor will go up in order to pay for the war (p. 55), and husbands, brothers and sons come back wounded. One of Jussup's neighbours sums it up succinctly, as part of the general practical wisdom the peasants have acquired: 'The leaders on one side can win a war, the soldiers on both sides lose it' (p. 55). In the

'Mother Grusinia' court case, the bandit brings the old woman the cow to ensure her livelihood 'because your son has been killed in the war' (p. 80), and Azdak calls her 'The Bereaved Mother/Whose sons have gone to war' (p. 81). And at the end of Scene 4 we are told that as the 'area of disorder' ends with the return of the Grand Duke and the Governor's wife, 'the people's quarters burned anew' (p. 82) – once again, those paying for the conflict are the lower classes.

One major theme in this play is the need for change and the difficulty of bringing it about. War is clearly not the way – the lower classes suffer while the rulers and the privileged compete for power.

After the two years with Azdak as judge, the social order has not been significantly affected or improved. That is why Azdak's reign was 'golden' but also 'brief'. There has been no fundamental revision of society and justice, but '*Almost* an age of justice' (p. 99). At first it appears as if things will go back to the previous situation: while the Governor is dead (as is the Fat Prince), the Grand Duke is back in power and the Governor's wife (now widow) is confident that her power and possessions will be restored to her. And yet, in a number of individual cases (of which we see a total of five), Azdak has seen to it that the poor and unprivileged are given a chance. And, in the case of Michael, he has gloriously managed to unmask the greed and cold-heartedness of those in power and rendered a verdict that both awards Michael to the only mother he has ever known and rewards Grusha for what she has done.

The thematic core of the play is the question of what it means to be a mother and much of the play can be read as an attempt to redefine that meaning. Grusha's motherliness and her love for Michael develop out of responsibility and shared hardship. As a result of the very sacrifices that she makes for him, Michael becomes precious to her. We should remember that after

Conclusion: Major Themes and Overall Interpretation

hearing the silent song the baby sings to her, she does not move immediately to take care of him. The song merely motivates her to sit and wait with him a little longer. She 'sat too long' until the 'seduction was complete' (p. 29) – another odd assessment of what has happened, by way of which Brecht wants to emphasize that Grusha is not making a noble, informed decision. By the time she adopts him, however, she knows exactly what she is getting into. This is in stark contrast to the initial exaggerated fussing of his birth mother that quickly turns into negligence under the pressure of a situation Natella Abashwili is wholly inadequate to cope with.

When we compare this play to the two sources from which Brecht derived his central motif, the Chinese *Chalk Circle* legend and King Solomon's decision in the Bible (see Introduction), Azdak's judgement deviates in one crucial respect. In both the Chinese and biblical versions, it is the natural mother, the mother tied to the child by birth, who turns out to be the 'true' mother. Brecht teases apart that unquestioning convergence of biological and emotional-social motherhood. In his play, the birth mother is a mother only in name and the 'bonds of blood' are meaningless. Azdak teaches us that asking who 'is' the actual mother is the wrong question; instead, we need to see how someone acts, and motherliness is proven by actions. The 'true' mother, then, is not the biological mother but the adoptive mother who raised and cared for the child.

Grusha redefines motherhood and the play makes a strong case for us to agree with her, as does Azdak. Two of the songs in particular affirm the power of motherhood as understood by Brecht: Grusha's song at the end of Scene 2 (pp. 42–3), which predicts that her son will be kind and gentle because she will instil those values in him; and her silent response (articulated by the Singer) to Azdak's question whether it would not be preferable for the child to grow up rich (p. 96). Grusha, in other words, may not be Michael's natural mother, but becomes all the more truly his mother through her actions. In spite of her low-key and unsentimental way of talking about him, by the end there can be no doubt that she loves him as her child, even though she studiously avoids such emotional terms as 'love' or 'bond', which are invoked so freely by the Governor's wife and her lawyers. In fact, one of the many lessons the play can offer us would be suspicion towards flowery and emotional rhetoric.

Azdak's verdict is symbolic on several levels. It provides justice in a complex situation and it offers us a way of assessing and working towards justice and, beyond that, towards a more equitable distribution of assets and responsibilities in society. We may regard it as a small but nonetheless institutional move towards change: the child has been given to the mother who deserves him, and the Governor's estate, the fruit of high rank, private enrichment and an abuse of power, is given over to a new use as a public space for children. Will his final verdict lead to more change, or will this simply remain Azdak's legacy as he fades into legend?

Brecht leaves us with that question, but also with the final lines that seem so simple and logical and yet question how well the world works. While Grusha, Simon and Michael will presumably be happy together, the relatively open end of the play is not quite a fairy tale with regard to the bigger picture. Although it refers us back to the Prologue with its optimistic scene of debate and peaceful agreement celebrated with art, the play as a whole encourages us to continue to think more critically about social justice and what it will take to build a better world for everyone.

Discussion Topics and Examination Questions

Your understanding and appreciation of the play will be much enhanced if you discuss aspects of it with other people. Here are some topics you could consider:

- How important is the revolutionary setting for what happens in the play?
- Would you consider Azdak corrupt? Why – or why not?
- Where does Brecht's technique of distancing us from the characters work? Are there places where it breaks down and you identify strongly with a character?
- How does Brecht use food in this play? What role does it have in individual scenes?
- While this play as a whole is not a comedy, where does Brecht employ comedy in individual scenes? What effects does it have on us?
- Where does Brecht make use of contradictions? Which characters show them most clearly?
- How does the final scene show sincerity and insincerity? How do you feel about Grusha's statement, and about the lies offered by the cook and Simon?

General examination questions

You may find that the texts chosen by your teacher have been selected from a wide set of suggestions in the examination syllabus. The questions in the examination paper will therefore be applicable to many different books. Here are some questions which you could answer by making use of *The Caucasian Chalk Circle*:

- Choose a work that presents a family and show what is characteristic about this family, what holds it together and how it develops.
- Write about a novel or play you know where a character has to make a difficult decision that involves sacrifice.
- How can the staging of a play affect our interpretation? Using a play you have read, discuss what choices a director can make and what their effect would be on us as spectators.
- Choose any play or novel you have studied in which minor characters affect the action of the plot significantly. Identify at least two of the characters in the work you have chosen and explain how their roles in the plot are important.
- Choose a play or novel and explain how the language in which the characters express themselves contributes to our impression of them and to the overall significance of the work.
- Novels and plays are often said to have 'heroes'. Do these heroes always have to act in heroic and courageous ways? Choose a text, discuss one or more characters who may or may not act heroically, and

examine the concept of 'heroism' using them as examples.

Examination questions on *The Caucasian Chalk Circle*

- How important are class distinctions in this play? Give examples of how belonging to a certain class shapes the statements, opinions and actions of characters.
- Is the Prologue necessary or should it be omitted in contemporary stage productions of the play? Choose one position, or give reasons for both positions.
- How does the plot of the play differ from the classical European model (in three or five acts) and why?
- How does Brecht define and show motherliness in this play? Explain how and why his play is different from the sources he used in his view of motherhood.
- Why has Azdak, one of the two main characters, been called 'the good bad judge'? Discuss the different ways in which one can characterize and assess his performance as judge.
- What functions does the Singer perform? Why is he so important?

Notes

Notes

Notes

Notes

Notes

Notes

Notes

Notes

Notes

Notes

Notes

Notes